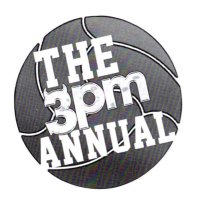

THE STUPIDEST
FOOTBALL
BOOK EVER

First published in 2010. A catalogue record for this book is available from the British Library

ISBN: 978-0-857330-39-0

Published by Haynes Publishing, Sparkford, Yeovil, Somerset BA22 7JJ, UK
Tel: 01963 442030 Fax: 01963 440001 Int. tel: +44 1963 442030 Int. fax: +44 1963 440001
E-mail: sales@haynes.co.uk Website: www.haynes.co.uk

Haynes North America Inc., 861 Lawrence Drive, Newbury Park, California 91320, USA

All images © Mirrorpix

Creative Director: Kevin Gardner

Designed for Haynes by BrainWave

Printed and bound in the US

THE STUPIDEST
FOOTBALL
BOOK EVER

STEVE ANGLESEY

FOREWORD
BY ROBBIE SAVAGE

If you only buy one book this year, make it *Savage! The Autobiography of Robbie Savage* (Mainstream, £17.99, available at all good bookshops now).

If you only buy two books this year, you could do worse than make the second one this offering from my pal Steve Anglesey.

There are some hilarious football stories in these pages, although I'm staggered to see that my missus Sarah hasn't made it into Steve's list of The 100 Maddest People in Football.

This is the woman who once asked me when she would meet our new signing Og (she'd seen on Teletext that we'd won a game thanks to an own goal). Who ran a raffle at our kids' school and asked me how much she'd get if she sold all 300 tickets at £1 each. Who looked at an unintelligible menu in the poshest restaurant in Italy and asked for help as she couldn't speak French.

Who said we shouldn't take the kids' cricket set on a beach holiday because we wouldn't be able to stick the stumps in the sand. Who bought our lad an XXS England goalie shirt with the keeper's name on the back and explained that the size was "two times small" but she was worried that everyone would think his name was James. Who took a picture of our two boys, Charlie and Freddie, and said: "It's amazing – anyone who didn't know them would think they were related."

It's a good job she's so fit.

Of course, you'd know all these stories already if you read my brilliant column in the *Daily Mirror* every Friday.

Steve's got a column in the paper too, every Monday, from which many of these stories are taken. It's almost as good as mine.

Robbie Savage, Derby
August 2010

AUTHOR'S NOTE

"Now, I love old radio stories. And I know a million of 'em. I've collected 'em down through the years, like a hobby. Anecdotes and gossip... and inside stories about the stars."

These lines from the start of Woody Allen's *Radio Days* pretty much sum up this book. I've been collecting weird football stories and facts for years now, and the best make it into my 3PM column in the *Daily Mirror* every Monday. Some of my favourites from the last decade are spread over these pages. But it would be remiss of me not to include the anecdote that started all this off.

Years ago, I met a policeman who'd once stopped a flash car for speeding. When the driver rolled down his window, the copper was surprised to see the sheepish face of a very famous England international.

Naturally, he was asked to produce his licence. "I can't, I'm afraid," said the player. "They took it off me in Wolverhampton."

The policeman was baffled. What?

"They took it off me in the court in Wolverhampton a month ago," confirmed our hero. "I'm banned from driving in Wolverhampton for a year."

The ensuing conversation made it clear that this household name, who'd been stopped for speeding on his way to a match and had accumulated the necessary points, actually believed that his driving ban extended no further than the Tuscany of the West Midlands. Since he was now in Birmingham, he had presumed he was all-clear to drive.

The policeman was so stunned by this he decided to let him go and we can only presume that the midfielder spent the next 12 months skirting the environs of Wolverhampton, eager not to break the conditions of his ban.

I'd like to thank him and all the footballers who appear in this book. Thanks too to Robbie for the Foreword, Dave Tarbox and Mirrorpix for the illustrations and photographs and to Richard Havers and to Jeremy Yates-Round at Haynes. To Dean Morse and Howard Johnson and to everyone who has contributed items to 3PM down the years (send your stories and tips to mirror3pm@hotmail.com), most notably the *Daily Mirror*'s brilliant staff of reporters. To my dad for dragging me into football and my mum for dragging me into journalism. And especially to Mel, Eve and John for putting up with me in the rare moments when there's not a match on.

Canary Wharf
August 2010

THE 100 MADDEST PEOPLE IN FOOTBALL

Every week my 3PM column brings you amazing true tales of players, fans and administrators at their most insane. Here's a countdown of my favourite characters and stories...

No. 100 MANCHESTER CITY'S TATTOOED FANS

Confident his beloved Blues would finish in the top four at the end of the 2009/10 campaign, Kirk Bradley decided to have the "Manchester City 2011 Champions League Winners" tattooed on his arm. Alas, City ended up fifth and in the Europa League instead. Undaunted, our hero declared he would have the date altered to 2017 and tattooist John Logan said: "Kirk has got to be one of the most optimistic fans going."

Another is Chris Atkinson, who on hearing of City's interest in Kaka, went straight out and had the Brazilian's name tattooed across his chest. Alas, the God-fearing midfielder went to Real Madrid instead. "The lads in the pub thought it was a transfer at first but when I showed them it was real they just laughed," said "gutted" Chris.

No. 99 JERMAINE JENAS

Not always sure of a place in Tottenham's first team, the midfielder at least has established himself as a regular in the style

pages, where he can be found posing (usually topless), showing off tattoos including the profound "It's Easier To Destroy Than Create" (in Latin, naturally), admitting to owning leather jackets in red, green and blue and calling his Blackberry "an extension of me".

Asked to name the last time he had been on public transport, Jenas replied: "When I went back to Nottingham about a year ago, they had recently started a tram service around the city. My mates and I thought it would be a bit of a laugh just to jump on a tram and see what happened." The tram went to the next stop presumably.

More recently he has become a gossip mag favourite alongside girlfriend Ellie Penfold, who says: "The best present Jermaine ever got me is priceless – a tattoo of my face on his forearm. He always chooses the most thoughtful things."

No. 98 SHAUN RYDER

9

The self-medicating Happy Mondays and Black Grape genius is a staunch critic of the American Old Trafford takeover.

An interviewer asked: "The opposition to the Glazer family is well known. As a United fan, is Shaun Ryder now wearing green and gold rather than red and white?" Shaun replied: "No. But I might be if, you know, I had a green and gold scarf."

No. 97 TIM LOVEJOY

"The hardest thing about leaving *Soccer AM* is the thought that I might no longer be influencing the game," wrote modest Lovejoy in his autobiography, before going on to influence the game of cooking on live TV of a weekend morning while playing some old TV clips. The former Watford supporter turned Chelsea fan – he moaned after the Blues' Champions League exit in 2009 that "Barcelona are so one-dimensional, they only know one way of playing" – is now only a peripheral figure in the game he once bestrode like a colossus, having missed out on replacing Adrian Chiles on *MOTD2* and lost his stint on Radio Five Live's *Six-O-Six*, where he would regularly admonish callers who dared to suggest that England's players might not actually walk into any team in the world.

Still, we'll always have the 38 pictures of himself in his autobiography – as Ally Ross has pointed out, this is eight more photos than there are of Nelson Mandela in *The Long Walk To Freedom*.

No. 96 HERMANN HREIDARSSON

The Premier League defender took the phrase "international break" a bit too literally while on Iceland duty. Revealed a team-mate: "Hermann had enough

THE 3pm ANNUAL

of warming up so asked the assistant manager Petur Petursson how much longer it was going to be. Petursson told him two minutes so for a bit of banter Hermann ran up and tackled the coach from behind. The X-rays came back with news Hermann had broken the guy's collar bone."

No. 95 MARK HALSEY

When he's not refereeing, Halsey can be found greeting customers in Sottovento, the Italian restaurant he owns near Bolton. One customer asked him to give Manchester United a penalty the next time he was at Old Trafford. Quipped the ref: "Well, the missus is a red – if I don't give you anything, I don't get any sex."

11

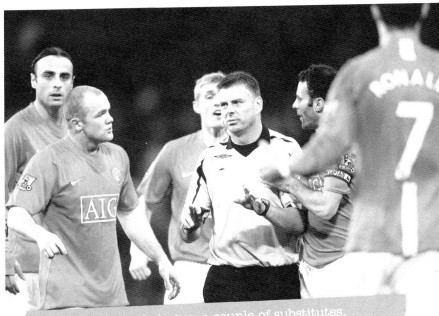

No. 94 ANDREY ARSHAVIN

When he arrived at Arsenal with his high-pitched Russian accent, Arshavin was immediately dubbed 'The Meerkat', in tribute to the Compare the Market TV advert. A deep thinker who believes that soon "they will put a camera in a footballer's pants in order to get a story", Andrey has recently become an agony aunt to readers of his website. Here he tackles thorny questions like "have you ever been stung by the bees around the eyes?" and used the wisdom of Solomon to conclusively settle this query:

Q: Hi, Andrey, in what order would you place the following animals: a tiger, a cow, a pig, a horse, a sheep?

Arshavin: A pig – it will always get the last place. A tiger, a cow, a horse, a sheep. And I'll repeat that a pig is always the last one, because it is a pig.

No. 93 DANNY MURPHY'S FAMILY

Fulham's former Liverpool midfielder is a no-frills type. Not so his yoga-teaching, hippy half-brother, who has changed his name to Luos... because it is "soul" spelt backwards.

Meanwhile, Murphy's actress wife Joanna briefly wrote a newspaper column which she began by insisting, "it's not all high glamour being a footballer's wife." Unglamorous topics covered turned out to include her honeymoon in Barbados, Michael Owen's "wonderful house with beautiful stables", the "five-star hotel" where she stayed while visiting the Taj Mahal, Steven Gerrard's "beautiful villa in Portugal" and this moan about curtailed holidays: "We had so many plans for this summer, but they had to be scrapped when I got a part in a film that I've just finished with Martin Kemp and Dennis Waterman."

No. 92 FLYBE'S MIKE RUTTER

Fans cried when Portsmouth went into administration in 2010 accepting a 15-point penalty which virtually relegated them on the spot. Within minutes of the announcement budget airline Flybe saw the chance for some cheap publicity and won the oxymoron award for corporate sensitivity by issuing this press release:

"Flybe will welcome Premiership stars from crisis-club Portsmouth FC on board today as the team takes advantage of the airline's low fares to fly to Manchester for their six-pointer against Burnley at the weekend. Flybe can confirm media reports that the club bagged great value flights on its popular Southampton to Manchester service." Mike Rutter, Flybe's Chief Commercial Officer said: "Flybe is pleased to welcome Pompey's players on board today as following the news of their administration. It's pretty clear that Flybe can fly you to your destination with the minimum of fuss and for a great price."

No. 91 JAMES CORDEN

Adored for his series *Gavin & Stacey* and loved for his previous, Lovejoyesque, TV work with footballers, giving Corden a football-themed show during the 2010 World Cup must have seemed a no-brainer to ITV. Alas, what was billed as "the ultimate summer-long party" led to a witless whoopfest and the biggest reversal of fortune for an overweight comedian since Virginia Rappe met Fatty Arbuckle.

The die was cast in the opening moments of the first show, which went as follows:

CORDEN: "Gordon Banks, is it true that England drew their first match in 1966?"
BANKS: "Yes, it's true, we did draw 1-1 against Uruguay. But we went on to win in 1966 – Geoff Hurst scored a hat-trick."
SIMON COWELL: "Gordon, hi, it's Simon. Gordon, I hope I'm not being rude, but is it true that we, England, drew our first match in 1966? But we went on to win the tournament that year...? Didn't we? That is, England?"
BANKS: "Simon, we drew our first match in 1966, and there was a lot of criticism in the press, but we went on to win the World Cup that year – in 1966 – with Geoff Hurst scoring a hat-trick in the final against Germany."

Another moment: asking Peter Crouch, "Before a game, when you're waiting in the tunnel do you ever have a sniff of the other side to see if there are any you don't fancy swapping shirts with afterwards?"

Corden later claimed Fabio Capello should have made the World Cup: "More of a laugh." Pot, meet kettle.

13

CONTINUES
P22

PUZZLE TIME

How many words related to Manchester United's popular manager can you find hidden in the grid?

	A	B	C	D	E	F	G	H	I	J	K	L	M	N	O	P
1	S	S	S	F	E	I	R	L	B	F	U	H	S	O	E	E
2	I	U	I	E	M	A	G	D	N	I	M	R	R	R	R	R
3	N	O	S	U	G	R	E	F	X	E	L	A	R	I	S	A
4	T	I	A	B	U	R	G	U	N	D	Y	R	T	R	P	U
5	I	C	N	N	T	H	A	I	R	D	R	Y	E	R	U	N
6	M	A	B	R	N	L	C	C	E	I	E	A	B	I	S	C
7	I	R	A	B	U	S	I	V	E	T	I	L	O	P	M	I
8	D	G	B	I	L	C	H	U	R	L	I	S	H	I	T	V
9	A	N	R	H	B	U	O	I	B	I	E	M	C	B	A	I
10	T	U	H	C	T	A	W	P	O	T	S	E	S	D	L
11	I	G	P	F	Y	A	I	E	I	E	O	U	S	I	G	L
12	N	S	T	L	G	D	R	F	N	E	Q	R	O	N	N	R
13	G	N	U	O	U	C	D	F	S	S	N	T	I	U	P	I
14	P	S	V	R	H	U	T	U	U	V	S	E	E	S	S	T
15	G	A	B	I	L	N	O	R	R	D	G	L	E	S	H	T
16	N	R	I	D	T	Y	B	G	E	A	D	G	S	U	E	L

14

WORDS TO FIND

SIRALEXFERGUSON
ABRUPT
ABUSIVE
HAIRDRYER
BLUNT
BOORISH
CHURLISH
GRACELESS
GRUFF

IMPOLITE
SURLY
UNCIVIL
UNGRACIOUS
BRUSQUE
RUDDY
FLORID
GOVAN
AGEING
YOUSE

PERCH
IDIOTS
BBC
STOPWATCH
BURGUNDY
INTIMIDATING
FERGIETIME
MINDGAMES

Answers Page 159

THE 50 MADDEST
FOOTBALL VIDEOS... EVER

Want to watch Saturday's goals from the Premier League, last night's Championship highlights or the latest 0-0 draw from Serie A? Then use your telly. *MirrorFootball.co.uk's* daily 3PM Extra feature brings you the real football highlights –wall-to-wall fainting commentators, mass brawls, brave attempts to speak a foreign language and the occasional pissed manager. Enjoy our selection of the 50 best we've featured so far, courtesy of the miracle of YouTube...

50) Jamie and Louise Redknapp's Thomas Cook spoof ad

As multi-millionaires, whenever Jamie Redknapp takes the lovely Louise on holiday it's always a package job from Thomas Cook. At least, that's what they asked us to believe in a 2009 telly advert during which Jamie – a top, top actor –

15

showed off his penchant for topless golf. Luckily, pranksters were on hand to strike back...
Search for "Redknapp Thomas Cook advert" or go to http://bit.ly/9WMQzo

49) Rival commentators at the Milan derby

One of them supports Milan. One of them supports Inter. And when they met, it was moider...
Search for "funny Italian football commentators" or go to http://bit.ly/cuGfYC

48) Hristo Stoichkov speaks in tongues

Bulgarian genius Hristo "The Dagger" Stoichkov could turn his hand to most things. Learning English during his stint at South Africa's Mamelodi

Sundowns wasn't one of them. Among the highlights: "The first team believe in glorification. First half good, second half I'm not right. No work. No sacrifissee, this is the team."

Search for "Stoichkov interview English" or go to http://bit.ly/7lgla9

47) Mesut Ozil: Gumthing special

Germany's World Cup star might have the eyes of Kermit, but he's got the skills of Maradona, as proved by this bit of chuddy-juggling from South Africa.
Search for "Ozil gum juggling" or go to http://bit.ly/b4CqEj

46) 'Arry Redknapp not 'appy

One of the all-time greats, this. Fans are used to seeing the genial side of Redknapp as he deals out Cockernee wisdom and cheerfully chats about how much he admires other teams' players.

But being clobbered by a ball in training makes him as mad as a property slump in Sandbanks...
Search for "Redknapp hit with ball" or go to http://bit.ly/4Bs5Ad

CONTINUES
P28

50 GREATEST MOMENTS
IN WAGDOM

While England's footballers serially disappoint on the pitch, their wives and girlfriends rarely do as they continue to amuse and delight in Britain's boutiques and nightclubs...

1) In 2006, arch-WAG Danielle Lloyd competed in an online version of TV game show *Test the Nation*. Asked: "Who was Winston Churchill: A rapper; US President; The PM; King" she replied: "Wasn't he the first black president of America? There's a statue of him near me – that's black." Alas, Danielle had been confused by the black marble statue of Winnie near her home in Woodford Green, Essex. She later explained: "I was planning on going to university until I won Miss England. Believe it or not, I wanted to be a forensic scientist."

17

2) Amaia Salamanca, ex-WAG of Real Madrid stars Sergio Ramos and Guti, stars in a Spanish TV show called *No Paradise without Tits*.

3) *Celebrity Big Brother* WAG Nicola T used

to have a six-foot blow-up photograph of her breasts above the bed she shared with Bobby Zamora. The couple split when Bobby gave her only a cheque for her birthday.

4) When blonde WAG Charlotte Mears moved in with Jermain Defoe she persuaded the England striker to spend £200,000 on a state-of-the-art kitchen with six ovens and two dishwashers – despite being unable to cook.

Charlotte later confessed: "I wasn't very good at following recipes but managed spaghetti and lasagna. I found the equipment difficult to operate, though. It was all touch-screen and all I wanted to do was turn an old-fashioned button. Sometimes I couldn't even turn the hotplate on and ended up breaking my manicured nails. It wound me up."

5) Charlotte celebrated her split from Defoe by having a boob job – even though she has a phobia of balloons.

6) In a 2007 *Daily Mirror* interview, Charlotte answered trivia questions. Her answers revealed that she thought Margaret Thatcher was the Queen, that World War II took place in either 1911 or 1852, that J K Rowling wrote *Wuthering Heights* and that the Berlin Wall was built to separate Germany and Russia. Charlotte also believed that New York was the capital of the

"Fraizer Campbell has two great feet... left and right." – **MARK BRIGHT**

USA. Heather Swan, then the WAG of Michael Chopra, corrected her by

pointing out that it was, in fact, Texas.

 19

⁊) Only three weeks after their wedding on Friday 13th June 2008 Heather and Chopra split up. She said: "We had a fantastic day and I wouldn't change that." Heather and Chopra's wedding included an ice sculpture of an angel which doubled as a vodka dispenser.

8) Michael Carrick's wife is called Lisa Roughhead – the

"Man City have scored in all of their home wins this year." – ROB HAWTHORNE

best WAG name since snooker's Stephen Hendry married the former Mandy Tart.

9) WAGdom's finest hour came at the 2006 World Cup, when the girls colonized the quiet, upmarket German town of Baden-Baden. A six-WAG team was said to have spent £57,000 on clothes and shoes in one shop alone and on their last day in Baden-Baden, our girls blew £30,000 in a single afternoon at the Monika Scholz boutique. Meanwhile, the WAGs rolled up almost £600,000 in hotel bills and room service at the plush Brenner's Park Hotel. Frank Lampard's then missus Elen Rives clocked up an extras bill of £28,607.

10) Victoria Beckham is rumoured to travel with three different sizes of the same pair of jeans "in case she loses weight" on the trip.

CONTINUES
P42

THE 3pm ANNUAL

THE 100 MADDEST PEOPLE IN FOOTBALL
CONTINUED

No. 90 ZAK ANSAH

One Manchester United supporter was so chuffed by their demolition of the
Gunners in 2009 that he posted this on Facebook: "United fans H8 Arsenal.
All you gassed up Arsenal fans who fought dey could bring it to United need
to pipe down... Arsenal fans lemme know how we cut your defence open,
Rooney fort it was Christmas!

I support United and don't like the way their was no English players in
the starting 11 against us! United fans H8 Arsenal." The writer? Highly-rated
youth footballer Zak Ansah, who plays for Arsenal's U-16s and is tipped to
break into the first team.

No. 89 JI-SUNG PARK

Manchester United's South Korean has been dogged (sorry) by Old
Trafford chants concerning his country's cuisine. These include a version

22

"Preston have an overpass in the middle of the
pitch." – STEVE COTTERILL

of '10 Green Bottles', which goes: "Ten Alsatians, walking down the street. Ten Alsatians, walking down the street. And if Ji-Sung Park fancies one to eat, There'll be nine Alsatians, walking down the street." There's also this reworking of 'Lord of the Dance': "Park, Park, wherever you may be. You eat dogs in your home country. But it could be worse, you could be Scouse. Eating rats in a council house."

Dubbed 'Three-Lung Park' for his tireless running, the midfielder is also tirelessly eccentric. Korean TV viewers have seen him vomit after eating a chocolate-covered insect as a prank, and celebrate his birthday by having former team-mate Carlos Tevez fire party poppers into his eye, causing severe swelling. Last season reporters on a United plane back from a European match noticed him sitting happily while team-mates including Patrice Evra beat him on the head with a sandal.

No. 88 GRAHAM POLL

The former referee now opens his after-dinner speeches with the words: "Good evening, I'm the prat who gave one player three yellow cards at the World Cup." Hertfordshire resident Poll opened his autobiography *Seeing Red* by thanking "the people of Tring for their quiet solidarity", raising the intriguing possibility that the people of Tring had simply been ignoring him.

He is now a newspaper pundit whose column has included wisdom like: "There is a saying in refereeing, 'You'll never see a racehorse refereeing a match.'"

No. 87 WEST HAM'S ANTIPODEAN FAN

West Ham upped the ante on pre-match entertainment last season, treating fans to a kids'

party bubble machine and a tape of Cockernee favourites including 'Knees Up Mother Brown' and 'Roll Out the Barrel'.

But this was a mere appetizer for the day a supporter who had flown in from Australia just to watch the Hammers was introduced to the crowd. He was naturally asked, "What made you, as an Aussie, support West Ham?" Replied our Antipodean chum: "It was after I saw the hooligans on the film *Green Street*."

No. 86 **ABBY NEVILLE**

The 20-year-old Manchester United fan from Bristol signalled the impeding apocalypse by arriving for the 2007 FA Cup final sporting Ugg boots, a Fendi handbag and Dolce & Gabbana glasses and proudly telling the *Sunday Times*: "The FA Cup final has become a social event in the calendar which whole families now are coming to."

No. 85 **ALAN SHEARER**

Match of the Day's fun-loving pundit has long been a favourite of interviewers for his jocular style and willingness to send himself up. A recent example from the *Guardian*:

Q: When you were a youngster what was your favourite cartoon?

A: Cartoons? I didn't watch cartoons, I was too busy playing football.

Q: Apart from a football, did you have a favourite toy when you were a child?

A: Yes, a goalpost.

Q: Apart from football paraphernalia, did you have a favourite toy when you were a child?

A: No, like I told you I was too busy playing football.

24

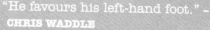

"He favours his left-hand foot." - **CHRIS WADDLE**

"To think of John Terry leaving is unthinkable." – **JASON CUNDY**

Q: What is your favourite vegetable?

A: What type of questions are these? I should say peas, should I?

Q: What about fruit?

A: An apple.

Q: You wouldn't have any time for an orange or a banana?

A: You asked for my favourite fruit, I said an apple.

Q: Do you believe in the existence of ghosts?

A: No.

Q: Do you believe in life beyond earth?

A: I don't know what I believe in. I try not to think about it. I don't want to think about it.

Q: Alan, can you tell us a joke?

A: Yeah, your questions.

No. 84 PETER STORRIE

The south coast's Peter Ridsdale led Portsmouth to FA Cup glory in 2008, financial disaster in 2009 and administration and relegation in 2010. Undaunted, he turned up to Wembley in a self-financed club suit to see Pompey beaten by Chelsea in the FA Cup final.

Storrie could afford it having picked up a £750,000 bonus in 2008 on top of his £450,000 basic. In 2009 the bonus was a mere £500,000 but his basic went up to £600,000.

Meanwhile, things were so bad at Fratton Park that when the club made its on-pitch presentation to its player of the month for January 2010, Asmir Begovic collected it while wearing the kit of opponents Stoke. He'd had to join them in Pompey's transfer window fire sale.

No. 83 STEPHEN BYWATER

Asked on a Sunday morning TV highlights show what advice he had received from his late mentor Les Sealey, the goalkeeper thought carefully, then said: "Don't be a See Yew Enn Tee to yourself", pausing over the initials to show how clever he was being. The ensuing fall-out saw Bywater banned from Sky Sports and presenter Clare Tomlinson disciplined.

According to his Derby room-mate Robbie Savage, Bywater wants to become a cage fighter when he retires.

"Tense and nervous are not the words, though they are the words." – CHRIS KAMARA

TONY CASCARINO

The player-turned-pundit once interrupted his *talkSPORT* show to punch co-host Patrick Kinghorn, who had made a cheeky remark about Cascarino's personal life. Studio staff then had to play trailers as the pair brawled on the office sofa.

But Cascarino's finest moment came in the 1990 World Cup, after Ireland were beaten by Italy. Then Prime Minister Charles Haughey visited the dressing room and Niall Quinn remembered: "Those of us brought up in Ireland stood there in amazement as he made a speech about sporting sons of Ireland. It was totally hair standing up on the back of the neck stuff. But not everyone was from Ireland. Tony Cascarino was behind me and said loudly: 'Who the f*** is that?', ruining the moment. I said: 'that's the Taoiseach'. Andy Townsend was beside him and said loudly again: 'Who is it, Cas?' And he said: 'Dunno. Quinny said he owns a tea shop.'"

YASSER AL QAHTANI

The striker lasted just one day on trial at Manchester City in 2008. Wrote former "mad" goalie turned Middle East football analyst John Burridge: "He flew into Manchester with a huge entourage, arrived at the training ground like a prince and when he took part in his first training session, his entourage lined the touchline cheering.

"When he got the ball, Richard Dunne smacked Al Qahtani with a 'welcome' tackle, and he fell on to the ground like a bag of chips. He started rolling around, squealing and had to be carried off the field."

CONTINUES P36

"They wear their hearts on their shirts." – STEVE BULL

THE 50 MADDEST FOOTBALL VIDEOS...
EVER CONTINUED

45) World Cup fan falls

It wasn't just England's reputation that took a giant tumble in South Africa. So did this supporter at Brazil's opening game against North Korea...
Search for "Great fall FIFA" or go to http://bit.ly/dw3XgG

44) Shocking penalty rebound miss

Not only is this American high school soccer game clanger a miss of Ronny Rosenthal proportions, it's accompanied by the perfect soundtrack – an incredulous crowd member screaming "What the f**k?"
Search for "Port Arthur penalty miss" or go to http://bit.ly/9O13cD

28

43) Peter Glaze v Hodgson

He looks like Liberace, sounds like Brian Walden and has the reputation as one of the game's calmest customers. Yet sometimes even Liverpool manager Roy Hodgson loses his rag – as he does in this vintage 1996 interview in which Italian TV pundit Maurizio Mosca – who looks suspiciously like *Crackerjack* legend Peter Glaze – has a pop at Woy for preferring Alessandro Pistone to Robert Carlos in defence.
Search for "Roy Hodgson Maurizio Mosca" or go to http://bit.ly/aPMd7h

42) Huge ball KO's kid

A 6ft student versus an 11ft-high ball.
There's only going to be one winner...
Search for "Huge soccer ball hits kid" or go to http://bit.ly/17AnK7

41) Beckham and Gary Neville hunt a wooden spoon

Another archive gem here as a young David Beckham nips round to his
mate Gary Neville's house for tea. David decides to make pasta in Gary's
kitchen but can't lay his hands on an important bit of equipment... although
the search does unearth the fact that
Gary has two drawers next to each other
which each contain a wooden spoon and
nothing else...
*Search for "David Beckham Gary Neville
kitchen" or go to http://bit.ly/17AnK7*

CONTINUES
P48

"I can sum up our performance in one word – passion
and desire." – **KEVIN BLACKWELL**

GAZZA **SORTS IT OUT**

Paul Gascoigne delighted the nation in July 2010 when he attempted to deliver lager, chicken and a fishing rod to suicidal gunman Raoul Moat. But, judging by these exclusive photographs, it's far from the first time kindly Gazza has intervened in a dangerous situation...

THE MOST DISTURBING
FOOTBALL PICTURE
EVER TAKEN

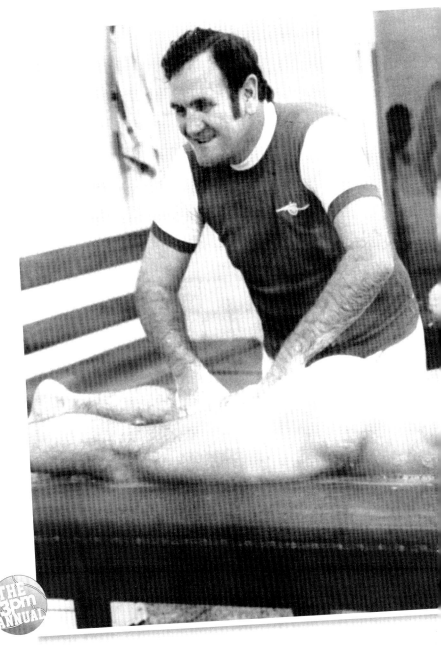

with the team to away games. However, once they were safely in the dressing room, he'd duck out of the stadium and head to the nearest pub for the afternoon, before returning to the team bus for the journey home.

Backpackers at a £10-a-night Thailand B&B were astonished to see veteran manager XXXXXXX XXXXXXXX in the check-in queue. All was explained when a steady stream of Ladyboys arrived at his door during an eventful one-week stay.

Pennywise star XXXXXXXXXXXXXXXX regularly appalls prospective conquests by making them split the bill at the end of the night, no matter how expensive the meal (often washed down with champers) was. He explains it's because "mum told me to watch out for gold-diggers now I've hit the big time".

XXXXXXXXXXXXXXX's reputation as a legendary swordsman is well founded. After one big-money move he was billeted by his new club in a posh local hotel but was ejected after a week. He'd taken a shine to one of the room service girls and ordered sandwiches at hourly intervals, always making sure to answer the door naked.

33

Sent to a rowdy pub to record a live edition of his show, radio pundit XXXXXXXXXXXXXXX threw himself into proceedings with such gusto that his station had to phone the landlord and order them not to serve the sozzled star any more drinks.

Scottish manager XXXXXXXXXXXXXX's players were delighted to discover that their manager was a regular at local grab-a-granny nights. In tribute, they began calling him "Jock McDogf***er".

XXXXXXXXXXXXXX's WAG is so obsessed with keeping her perfect smile that when the volcanic ash cloud stopped flights into Britain from Holland and threatened her dental appointment, she simply booked a taxi from Amsterdam to London instead.

CONTINUES P46

"I don't think you can say the title race is over, although realistically it is." – GAVIN PEACOCK

WICKED **WHISTLES**

Every week, my 3PM column features stories that make our lawyers nervous – so nervous, in fact, that they insist we disguise the names of the guilty parties. Here are some of the best...

Bad boy midfielder ~~XXXXXXXX XXXXXXXX~~ bet his club-mates that on a night out he could pull three different women who would fulfil different aspects of his sexual needs. His fellow players were amazed when, after only 20 minutes, he returned to the VIP area with a girl on each arm and introduced them as the "arse-tickler" and the "willy-pleaser". Ten minutes later he was spotted with a third girl and gestured to his friends that the hat-trick was on. But at the end of the night, he and the original two lasses were spotted glumly sitting by the door. "It's bad news lads," he told his team-mates. "The balls-fondler has gone home".

32

When he was arrested after some late-night shenanigans, police naturally searched ~~XXXXXXXX XXXXXXXX~~'s Louis Vuitton man-bag. Inside they were delighted to find a range of makeup which the sheepish star admitted to using to brighten his pasty complexion.

~~XXXXXXXX XXXXXXXX~~ had to discipline one of their top scouts after he was sent to check out a youth prospect in Europe. He took full advantage of the in-flight drinks, had a few at the hotel before the match and fell asleep in the first half on the shoulder of the youngster's mum. The kid signed for someone else.

While out with a long-term injury, ~~XXXXXXXX XXXXXXXX~~ impressed his coaches with his commitment by travelling

31

"Djourou, Owusu-Abeyie and the boy Smith... those three look a bit tasteful." – **CHARLIE NICHOLAS**

THE 100 MADDEST PEOPLE IN FOOTBALL CONTINUED

No. 80 RONNIE IRANI

Co-host (at the time of writing) of Alan Brazil's breakfast show, the former cricketer has impressed with his intelligence, asking Kenny Sansom: "This autobiography you've written... there's a lot of personal stuff in it, isn't there?" His finest moment is almost certainly the excitement with which he read out an email that had come from a listener far away in Rotterdam. Alas, it proved to have come from Rotherham instead.

No. 79 HARRY REDKNAPP

The loveable Cockney wheeler-dealer believes digital culture is stopping youngsters taking up the beautiful game. "Nowadays I rarely see a kickabout in the park," he said in 2007. "All I see are the dazzling lights of bedroom windows from the glare of TVs and computers. It seems football cannot compete with an Xbox."

A year later he returned to his theme, moaning: "Kids don't spend as much time playing football as they used to, they have other distractions, like computer games." 'Arry did his bit to turn the tide in 2010 by starring in adverts for Nintendo's Wii system and signing up to promote SEGA's Football Manager game.

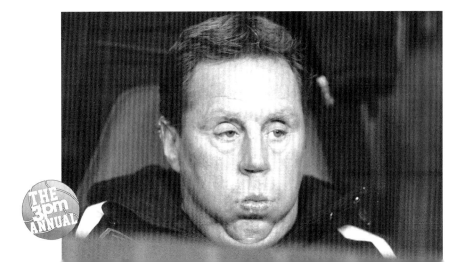

No. 78 **FRANK LAMPARD**

As conflicted as his Uncle Harry Redknapp, not-fat Frank saw nothing wrong with simultaneously heading up a child obesity campaign and appearing on adverts for Walkers Crisps.

No. 77 **KEVIN NOLAN**

When the combative midfielder signed up to provide a season-long diary of a professional footballer for the BBC Sport website, bosses presumably were expecting a no-holds barred account of life in the trenches from a fearless competitor. Instead, they got stuff like this:

"MONDAY: Had to be at training by the normal time. I got out of bed a little later than normal but managed to make it on time. The evening consisted of spending some time with the family and watching television.

"TUESDAY: I drive myself to training and enjoy the 40-minute journey. It gives me time to think and make a few phone calls – using the hands-free obviously. I have 10-15 tracksuits and wear one of these because I find them the most comfortable when I'm in the car.

37

"WEDNESDAY: I did a couple of interviews and then met my agent, who had come to watch the game. We chatted for about 30 minutes, during which time I drank some sparkling water.

"FRIDAY: After training we will travel down to Watford, then train and then transfer to our hotel. I always take my DVD player with me but most hotels we stay at have them – and anyway the telly is always quite good on a Friday evening."

Later, Nolan offered this gem: "Opposition fans often ask me where my sisters are. Just for the record, I don't have any sisters."

No. 76 JAMIE CARRAGHER

The short-fused Scouser, who came out of retirement to save England in South Africa to such spectacular effect, staked a convincing claim for Father of the Year honours by saying: "My son is six or seven years old and I'd love to take him to Wembley to watch Liverpool."

No. 75 CRISTIANO RONALDO

Photographed shortly after his arrival at Old Trafford holding his mother's hand to cross a busy Manchester street, Ronaldo later admitted that his favoured way of ridding himself of frustration after a rare bad game was to wedge a large TV set high in the branches of a tree, then kick footballs at it until it fell out.

He took this eccentricity to new levels after the World Cup, where he cheered himself up after Portugal's exit by producing a love child, naming it, naturally, Cristiano Ronaldo and then announcing he would be its sole carer. Then flying off to New York with his girlfriend – not the child's mother – and leaving the tot with his sister.

"Terry Venables looks younger with his little goatee... he's defining time." – **PAUL MILLER**

39

No. 74 AIDY BOOTHROYD

Dubbed "the David Brent of football", manager Boothroyd once described a player as "not fit physically or biomechanically". Other gems? "I don't want to settle for being a yo-yo club – I just want to be a 'yo' club"; "I believe in possible impossibles"; "We're always winners – even when we've lost"; "At this time of year, you get to see people like oranges – you squeeze them, and some tend to capitulate"; and "We grow our players at this club, we don't have a greenhouse in the back because we can't afford it, we're more of a microwave club."

However, all this is mere window-dressing for a tale from the latter stages of Aidy's Watford reign, when he bought an expensive radio receiver and microphone so he could watch events and dictate tactics from an Eagle's Nest on top of one of the stands. In the spirit of Spinal Tap, Boothroyd had to abandon the experiment when instead of

advice from his assistants, he began receiving requests for bedpans and hypodermic needles. Watford General hospital next door were using the same frequency.

No. 73 RACHEL STEVENS

The forgotten S Club mopsy burst back on to the scene in summer 2010, clad only in an England flag and strategically placed Cross of St George boater, as the face of Eau De Stade, "a new and exclusive unisex fragrance inspired by the scents of the beautiful game". Sold at £19.66 – geddit?! – the perfume was actually a stunt to draw attention to Sky Sports – a channel who had no World Cup live games and whose groundbreaking coverage of the final consisted of George Boateng sitting in front of a television monitor.

No. 72 NEMANJA VIDIC

Claimed to have been misquoted after a Russian magazine recorded him saying: "Manchester is the city of rain. Its main attraction is considered to be the timetable at the railway station, where trains leave for other, less rainy cities." Vidic hails from the Serbian city of Užice, whose main attraction is considered to be its copper rolling mill.

40

No. 71 DAVID PLEAT

"It's time for the Italians to say au revoir," declared Pleaty after the champions exited the 2010 World Cup finals. That adds to his legendary mispronunciations down the years. Here's a handy guide…

Pleaty says	Pleaty means
Benny Noon	Benayoun
Ronnie Deano	Ronaldinho
Evrice	Patrice Evra
Vieira	Vieri
Vieri	Vieira
Cliché	Clichy
Bennernoon	Benayoun
Radzinski	Rosicky
Dick Kurt	Dirk Kuyt
Astonbul	Istanbul
Jaynus	Jenas
Benjaynoon	Benayoun
Shimbomba	Chimbonda
Poil	Puyol
Ingazee	Inzaghi
Benny Ewing	Benayoun

41

CONTINUES
P50

50 GREATEST MOMENTS IN WAGDOM
CONTINUED

11) Nives Celcius, wife of Croatia's Dino Drpic, is famous for having sex on the centre spot of the Maksimir Stadium, Zagreb, where the Croats later beat England 2-0.

12) Stephen Ireland's WAG Jessica Lawlor drives a £290,400 Bentley. The Manchester City midfielder spent another £1,100 to change the car's legendary winged silver "B" logo to Jessica's initials "JL" and a further £2,200 on red leather seats with the message "To Jess, love from Stephen" stitched on to them. He then splashed out another £5,500 on bright red alloy wheel rims with Jess' initials to bring the total spend to an eye-watering £299,200.

13) While living with old man Teddy Sheringham, Danielle Lloyd had "Oh, Teddy, Teddy" as her ringtone. She changed it after they split following her *Celebrity Big Brother* bullying shame. Danielle denied that there was any racial element to her picking on Bollywood actress Shilpa Shetty and, coincidentally, soon began dating black footballers Marcus Bent and Jermain Defoe.

THE 3pm ANNUAL

THE 3pm ANNUAL

14) Wayne Rooney proposed to Coleen on a garage forecourt. After a row, she was later claimed to have thrown Wayne's £25,000 engagement ring into a squirrel sanctuary.

15) After Italy reached the 2006 World Cup semi-finals, Francesco Totti's wife Ilary Blasi moaned: "My heart is filled with joy at Italy's progress, but when will it end? I want Francesco back home so we can get on with extending our family. We are already way behind schedule."

16) Sven-Göran Eriksson's exotic WAG Nancy dell'Olio said of their first coupling: "It was a passion that set my soul on fire and made my body electric."

43

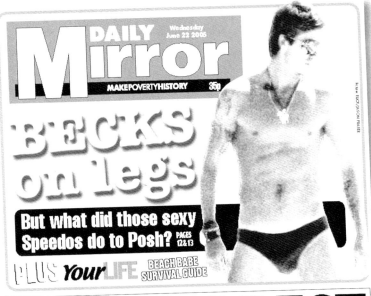

DAILY Mirror

Wednesday June 22 2005

MAKEPOVERTYHISTORY 35p

BECKS on legs

But what did those sexy Speedos do to Posh? PAGES 12&13

PLUS *Your*LIFE BEACH BABE SURVIVAL GUIDE

MY SEX PEST F.A. BOSS

Sven lover's shock claim

ACCUSER: Faria Alam yesterday and, right, Davies

By ALEXANDRA WILLIAMS

SVEN Goran Eriksson's ex-lover yesterday named FA boss David Davies as the third man in football's Sexgate Saga.

Faria Alam, 39, than Davies's PA, said the married former BBC reporter, 57, would try to kiss her in his office and in a lift.

She told of unwanted physical overtures. Miss Alam quit the FA after affair with England coach Eriksson and chief executive Mark Palios. It left the FA's reputation in tatters and cost Palios his job.

Miss Alam is now suing for constructive dismissal at an employment tribunal. Last night Mr Davies strongly refuted her allegations.

FULL STORY: PAGES 4 & 5

17) FA secretary turned after-hours WAG Faria Alam said Sven had surprise sex with her on the stairs of his Swedish hideaway. She reported: "It was very erotic, even if it did graze my knees."

18) Asked by Anne Robinson on a 2008 *Weakest Link* WAGs special, "In body shapes, the rhyming name sometimes given to a slightly flabby tummy is a jelly what?", *Big Brother* contestant and wannabe wag Charley Uchea answered, "fish".

"In his youth, Michael Owen was literally a greyhound." – **JAMIE REDKNAPP**

19) Dean Holdsworth and Mark Williams' ex-WAG Linsey Dawn McKenzie was asked: "In the animal kingdom, what H is the horny covering on each foot of a horse?" She replied: "Hall."

20) Cassie Sumner, who dated Michael Essien, was asked to name the "vegetable which has a variety called purple sprouting". Her answer? "Turnip".

CONTINUES P76

"He's already on a yellow card, so now he's really treading the boards." – **JOHN SALAKO**

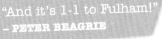
WICKED WHISTLES
CONTINUED

Referee ▓▓▓▓▓▓▓▓ is renowned as one of officiating's biggest posers. So much so that he admits to spending hours in front of the mirror practising giving out red and yellow cards in an attempt to "get my face right".

Beloved football administrator ▓▓▓▓▓▓▓▓ boasted that they lost their virginity to their sixth form pottery teacher – watched by fellow pupils from the comfort of the equipment cupboard.

Legendary hardman ▓▓▓▓▓▓▓▓ has got a serious drink problem. After disappearing from his pub's snug one night, regulars found him spark out in the communal urinal in the gents. They cleaned him up and sent him on his way, only to spot him outside the local chippy an hour later, eating chilli con carne with his bare hands.

Player-turned-coach ▓▓▓▓▓▓▓▓ is no longer allowed to speak to players at half-time after reducing one to tears with a finger-jabbing critique of his first-half play.

Scary manager ▓▓▓▓▓▓▓▓'s rants aren't being taken so seriously since he has taken to bollocking his players on the training ground while wearing a pair of comfy slippers on his feet.

Midfielder ▓▓▓▓▓▓▓▓'s ex-neighbours were delighted when he got a big-money move elsewhere. The girls, who lived in a flat downstairs, were tired of his creepy attempts to chat them up – which climaxed with them answering his knock at 10am on Sunday morning and opening the door to find him dressed in only his underpants, doing keepy-ups in the communal hallway!

46

"That's a tall ask."
– PHIL THOMPSON

Champions League goal machine XXXXXXXXXXXXXXXXXXXXX is a secret boozer. He defies the alcohol ban at his team's regular pre-match hotel by bribing staff to bring him bottles of lager, which he chugs down with them in the kitchen...

Supposedly loved-up XXXXXXXXXXXXXXXXXX is a four-timing cheat. He's cheating on his high-profile WAG with a nightclub barmaid, a hotel worker and an employee of his club.

Premier League giants XXXXXXXXXXXXXXXXXXXXX demanded that TV footage of their departure on a midweek "training camp" to Europe should be destroyed – as while their manager spoke of the gruelling practice sessions he had planned, his players could be seen in the background booking their golf clubs through check-in.

Homesick foreigner XXXXXXXXXXXXXXXXXX picked up English quickly. And that's not all he picked up after several night-time tours of his adopted northwest city's lay-bys and car parks.

Young star XXXXXXXXXXXXXXXXXXXX piled on the pounds so much over the summer that his club had to photoshop him out of the team photo and replace his head with one from the previous season.

A famous managerial name in the early days of the Premier League, XXXXXXXXXXXXXXX was also a nutter who would offer his team an incentive for away wins – he'd strip off on the coach and invite each member of the squad to punch him in the stomach.

Star defender XXXXXXXXXXXXXXXXXXXXXX pestered a female nightclubber for her mobile number so much that she got cheesed off and threw a drink over him. Our soaked hero then moaned: "Why did you have to do that? My wife bought me this top..."

CONTINUES P66

THE 50 MADDEST FOOTBALL VIDEOS... EVER CONTINUED

40) Wind scores own goal

Probably the most famous football YouTube clip ever. But there must be someone you know who hasn't experienced the simple joy of an unfortunate TSV Grunbach player inadvertently handing the lead to TSV Winsheim in a lower league game in Germany.

Search for "Wind own goal" or go to http://bit.ly/bRvBKO

39) Louis Van Gaal celebration fail

Remember José Mourinho's famous scamper up the Old Trafford sidelines after Porto knocked out Manchester United? Bayern Munich's Louis Van Gaal certainly does. But he's less of a Special One, more of a Right One...

Search for "Van Gaal fail" or go to http://bit.ly/cGm9eJ

38) Girlfight!

New Mexico Lobos defender Elizabeth Lambert became an internet sensation in 2009 after being filmed kicking, punching and pulling an opponent's hair in a college game against Brigham Young. You can see that video

by searching for her name or going to http://bit.ly/3CeEp6. But this scrap involving Lake Dallas and Denton Guyer high schools is even better. *Search for "Lake Dallas Denton Guyer" or go to http://bit.ly/azfh6X*

37) Mascot hits the post

Everyone loves a mascot race. Except, perhaps, for this now toothless lion. *Search for "Mascot hits post" or go to http://bit.ly/dmlzng*

36) Joachim's new Low

Germany coach Joachim Low's stock rose dramatically during the 2010 World Cup finals, thanks to his leggy Pop/Lux Interior looks and the way he and his spendidly named assistant Herr Flick co-ordinated their wardrobes. Shame he had to spoil it all with this dirty little habit.
Search for "Joachim Low nose" or go to http://bit.ly/ciEfKn

49

CONTINUES P64

THE 100 MADDEST PEOPLE IN FOOTBALL
CONTINUED

No. 70 SERGEI REBROV

The £11m flop striker enhanced his reputation in Tottenham still further by advising countryman and Spurs successor Roman Pavlyuchenko not to wander the streets of N17 because a "lot of dark skinned people live there". Rebrov later claimed he was merely passing on advice given to him by a taxi driver, in perhaps the best defence since Stan Boardman, caught in an Asian-baiting brouhaha at a Leeds United dinner, told Sky Sports News: "I'm not a racist. Some of my best friends are racists. Sorry, black."

"If you cut Jamie Carragher open, he'll bleed red." – CLIVE TYLDESLEY

"Jo has become a national hero on half of Merseyside." – **MIKE PARRY**

No. 69 'FANS' OF SHEPSHED DYNAMO

After starting their own website, non-league Shepshed Dynamo were astounded to find themselves receiving hundreds of thousands of hits from the United States. Alas, they quickly worked out that the spike in interest was not down to the Unibond First Division's growing profile in the USA, but related to internet searchers diverted there by mistake after typing in a couple of words found in the address of Shepshed's home ground: The Dovecote, Butt Hole Lane, Leicestershire.

No. 68 JEFF WINTER

The former referee is now a radio pundit and internet agony aunt, dispensing "hilarious" advice to his readers. A selection:

Here are a few highlights:

Q: Do you play Football Manager? If you're playing against a team who plays counter-attacking football would you think it's best to play defensively, hope they come out of their shell and hit them? Or should you play into their game plan and trust your players are good enough?

A: Get a fooking life. If you can't get a real woman, use your computer to find porn.

Q: Are homophobic comments acceptable in football, i.e. "Downing you big puff"?

A: Your pathetic example has pangs of schoolyard infantile name-calling. Funnily enough, Stuey's last bird looked OK to me.

Q: What's your favourite sport other than football?

A: Shagging.

51

No. 67 BOBBY SMITH

Spurs launched their £6,000 Opus photo-book by inviting double winner Smith on to the pitch before one match. Asked by the stadium announcer what he thought of the epic tome, our hero replied: "Well, it's six grand – who's going to want to spend that?"

"Both the keepers are suffering from confidence." – ALAN SHEARER

No. 66 **TONY HENRY**

Not the former Manchester City squad man, but the opera singer tasked with singing the Croatian national anthem before the infamous "wally with a brolly" game at Wembley. Instead of singing 'Mila kuda si planina' ('You know, my dear, how we love your mountains') Henry warbled 'Mila kura si planina' to the delight of the away fans. It means: "You know, my dear, my penis is a mountain".

No. 65 **ANDY JOHNSON**

The standing upright-adverse striker enlivened a dull programme Q&A with this exchange:

Q: Biggest passion outside of football?

A: I love nothing more than relaxing and spending time with my wife and son. I'm a family man.

Q: Which celebrity do you fancy most?

A: Carmen Electra.

53

"It's like trying to put a needle through a small hole." – **ALAN SMITH**

No. 64 RUPERT LOWE

With Southampton about to be relegated in 2005, the club's then chairman decided it was time to rally the troops via his programme column.

Supporters fretting about the team's perilous position were assured: "If the unthinkable happens and Saints are relegated, fans can see an extra four home games at no additional cost, at a comparable price to many comparable clubs in the Coca-Cola Championship." Churchillesque.

No. 63 TERRY VENABLES

Chirpy Cockney sparra turned Sadolin-skinned Martin Scorcese lookalike, Terry is setting himself up as a male Mystic Meg. Recent predictions include: "Without Ronaldo and Tevez, Manchester United will struggle" (they won the League Cup and finished second in the Premier League) and his uncanny view of the 2009 Champions League final: "Messi is wonderful on the right but Ronaldo is terrific on the right, the left and through the middle as well. He also scores goals with his head, which Messi couldn't do even if they put a top hat on him" (Messi scored a brilliant header; Ronaldo was anonymous).

No. 62 ANDRE GUMPRECHT

Eager to share a taste of his nation's history with team-mates at Australia's Central Coast Mariners, the German midfielder attended his club's fancy dress bash dressed as Adolf Hitler. He later explained that the costume "was meant in the spirit of fun". Not to be outdone, team-mate Tony Vidmar blacked up to go as Morgan Freeman.

No. 61 CARLOS BILARDO

After Argentina coach Diego Maradona told reporters that he would streak through the streets of Buenos Aires if Argentina won the World Cup, his

madder assistant upped the ante thus: "I say this: the player who scores our winning goal in the final is free to enter me from behind."

Bilardo guided the Albiceleste to World Cup glory in 1986 in remarkable fashion. He banned his players from eating chicken, believing it brought bad luck, carried a statue of the Virgin Mary to every match and insisted that newlywed brides were the key to success.

During the group stages in Mexico, the Argentinean bus broke down on their way to a match, resulting in the team having to take taxis to the game. The Argentineans duly won, with Bilardo making a correlation between the mode of transport and the victory. And that meant the team continued to flag down taxis before each game for the rest of the tournament.

During his time as coach of Estudiantes La Plata in 2003, a Brazilian woman wished Bilardo good luck ahead of a crucial game. After winning the match 4-1, he then instructed club officials to track down the woman before each game, and he would call her in order to secure any luck that might be going spare.

CONTINUES
P70

FOOTBALL'S MOST EMBARRASSING SPONSORS

West Ham briefly played with black patches over the logo of sponsors XL after the travel firm collapsed in 2008, leaving thousands of holidaymakers stranded. That was embarrassing. But not as embarrassing as these...

10) AC Milan: Pooh

The sponsors: 1960s band Pooh were dubbed "the Italian Beatles" before a quick-thinking jeans company squeezed in to nick the name. Their tie-up with Milan, which began in season 1981-82, is commonly reckoned to be the world's first shirt sponsorship.

Impact on the club: *Hardly flushed with success. Milan didn't win a thing of note until switching to the disappointingly normal Opel in the 1990s.*

9) FC Nürnberg: Mister Lady

The sponsors: Fittingly for Nürnberg, being sponsored by a clothes shop for teenagers proved a bit of a trial.
Impact on the club: *Relegated and promoted under Mister Lady in the last two seasons, the club is now backed by energy firm Areva.*

8) Denmark: Dong

The sponsors: The energy firm has sponsored the Danes since 2004, though their contract expires next season.
Impact on the club: *FIFA world ranking dropped from 15th to 38th under Dong, though has recently recovered to 26th.*

7) **Roma: Wind**

The sponsors: Italy's third-largest mobile phone company trumped rivals to become Roma's backers in 2007 and will carry on until the end of the season – when it will be Gone with the Wind.

Impact on the club: *Have been Serie A runners-up and Coppa Italian winners with the Wind at their backs (or fronts) but are currently in mid-table.*

6) **Clydebank: Wet Wet Wet**

The sponsors: Hairgel-loving local soul/popsters the Wets backed the Bankies from 1993 to 1997, the period which saw them spend 15 weeks at No.1 with 'Love is all Around' – eventually deleting the single to give someone else a chance – while frontman Marti Pellow developed a nasty heroin addiction.

Impact on the club: *Spent much of the sponsorship in the doldrums, then recorded a record low attendance of 29 in 1999 before going out of business in 2002. Now reborn in the lower leagues.*

5) Brighton: Nobo

The sponsors: Cocky suppliers of flip-chart easels and office products. Once had a board at the ground reading "Nobo Supports Brighton"; cheeky rivals allegedly added the letters d and y to the sponsors' name.

Impact on the club: *Relegated to Division Three in the second year of the sponsorship and remained there throughout, losing in the Wembley play-off final as Nobo shrunk away.*

4) Club America: Bimbo

The sponsors: Bimbo was the first Mexican firm to introduce sliced bread, which is colloquially known as "pan Bimbo" in the country. They've been backing Club America since 1995.

Impact on the club: *Though they're Mexico's richest side, Club America are decidedly not the best thing since sliced bread – they've not won the title with "Bimbo" on their shirts.*

58

3) Oxford United: Wang

The sponsors: Computer firm sponsored Robert Maxwell's side from 1985 to 1989. The Us then wore the name of Maxwell's academic books company, Pergamon Press, until the Fat Man went swimming in 1991. Wang fared about as well, filing for bankruptcy protection in 1992.

Impact on the club: *Won the League Cup as a promoted side in the first year of the sponsorship but, once Maxwell had lost interest after buying Derby County, were relegated in the final season.*

2) St Johnstone: Bonar

The sponsors: A local weaver of yarns for the carpet trade, the unfortunately named Bonar backed the Saints to celebrate their diversification into artificial turf. They've recently supplied useless NFL team the St Louis Rams with a new practice pitch.

Impact on the club: *As you'd expect from getting a Bonar, things went upwards for the Saints. They won the Scottish First Division in the first season of the sponsorship and reached the Scottish Cup semis (no giggling at the back) in its final year.*

And the most embarrassing shirt sponsor of all is...

1) Lyon: Le 69

The sponsors: They might have all but killed off Liverpool's Champions League hopes, but at least if the Anfield club had to sport their local dialling code on their shirts it'd only say 0151. In Lyon's case, things were slightly different in the early 1990s...

Impact on the club: *Despite their sniggersome sponsors, Lyon were promoted and consolidated in Ligune Une under handballer's pal Raymond Domenech – possibly because opponents were transfixed by their kit.*

PUZZLE TIME

Match the footballer with the kiss-and-tell quote.
Our heroes' nocturnal activities regularly land them in the Sunday tabloids. But can you match the player to the breathless testament to his horizontal abilities?

A: "We'd been to a nightclub but by the time we were back at my flat he was panting like a dog on heat. We tore our clothes off but he begged me to keep my corset on while I straddled him as he sat on the sofa. His stamina was amazing as you can imagine, being a footballer."

B: "He could barely speak English but I knew talking wasn't on his mind that night. We both moved to the bed and stripped each other. As he undressed me he looked at my thighs and gasped 'You, footballer' when he saw how toned they were. When I mimed riding a horse to show him how I got them that way it seemed to excite him all the more."

C: "We have never been an official item but we always meet up for drinks, to have a chat and to have sex. We've got a little halfway point in between where he lives and where I live. It's just off the M62 in between Leeds and Manchester. We come off the motorway and there's a little bridge near Rochdale so we just abandon my car and go for a drive in his. Maybe we stop off for a drink in a pub and do... whatever. It's really nice, it's not really mucky or horrible."

D: "The house was a massive pleasure palace. A waterbed covered in black silk sheets was on a raised area in the middle of the bedroom which he laughingly called his 'altar of love'. There was even a chrome pole beside it which he claimed was to support his television, but it looked suspiciously like one a poledancer would use."

E: "He was kissing me passionately all over my body and couldn't stop playing with my 34D boobs. One of the few English phrases he knew was 'I love your big t*ts' and he kept saying that. Sex was fast and furious. He was so excited he didn't last long."

F: "He only ever stripped me on the bottom half because he was too

THE 3pm ANNUAL

"I don't predict in football. But next week you will see a vastly different Norwich City." – **GLENN ROEDER**

"Grimsby could drop out of the league and go into obliviation." – **RONNIE IRANI**

impatient. He left my top and bra on, which was really strange. There was no foreplay and he just wanted to get straight on with it and had sex frantically for half an hour like a pneumatic drill. I couldn't believe it. He went at it hammer and tongs, like a teenage boy would."

G: "I was really shocked by his manhood. He had a great physique even though he is quite short. I thought he would have lots of stamina. He was also boring and I think he was a bit inexperienced. I wanted him to be naughty and adventurous but he wasn't. I was totally unsatisfied and he was utterly selfish. I was a bit embarrassed for him because he was so bad."

H: "He grabbed my bottom and started gently spanking me. The faster we went in our lovemaking the more he slapped my buttocks. He couldn't keep his hands off my bottom. He was obsessed with it. The longer we had sex the more he spanked me. It was amazing."

I: "It was pure, sweaty passion. He has massive legs and is very well endowed. He didn't have any body hair – anywhere. He was besotted with my boobs. It must be because Brazilian women are mad for plastic surgery but mine are all real. It was a change for him."

J: "He stole a kiss. It left me with a taste of onions so I had to have a soft drink, but no matter. This continued, then suddenly I heard a loud noise.

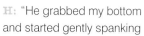

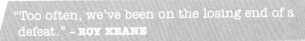

I thought it was the chair creaking. But no. He had broken wind."

K: "He slapped my backside so hard his wedding ring left an imprint. We started having sex but it wasn't long before he said he felt sick again. Then he just rolled over and vomited on the floor, all over the cream carpet. It was disgusting. He had some mouthwash, then jumped back into bed."

L: "I think the feel of a girl's wet hair against his body really turned him on because he couldn't get enough of the shower. He just couldn't keep his balance. We'd be about to have sex and then he'd slip. So we ran a bath instead. There was water everywhere at the end. But he kept falling over so we went to bed."

63

M: "Sex was so disappointing. He had been having problems with his ankle and was in and out of hospital having treatment. He was on top of me but every 30 seconds he had to stop to re-adjust his leg – it was really off-putting. I can only put his disappointing performance down to the medication he was on. The tablets must have had an effect on his manhood as it wasn't the biggest I've ever seen."

N: "I was struggling on crutches. He virtually carried me up the stairs to the toilets. We found an empty cubicle, sneaked inside and locked the door. He started kissing me and I think that was when he first noticed that I had my tongue pierced. He made the first move and undid his trousers. I think he was expecting it. He was very well endowed." Answers Page 159

"United have got Carrick, Scholes, Giggs, Owen Hargreaves
to come back, and then of course there's Benny Andersson."
– MICKY QUINN

"As the old saying goes, people in glasses shouldn't throw stones." – **ALAN SMITH**

THE 50 MADDEST FOOTBALL VIDEOS... EVER CONTINUED

35) Dog v Vuvuzela
Where did you stand on the great vuvuzela debate? This Pavlovia reaction shows the Swiss Mountain Dog vote is firmly paws down.
Search for "Dog vs vuvuzela" or go to http://bit.ly/apkdAc

34) German fan falls off car
Through gritted teeth, you've got to admit that Germany's poise and balance during the 2010 World Cup was very impressive. Alas, the same can't be said of this supporter.
Search for "German celebration goes wrong" or go to http://bit.ly/dAk1l3

THE 3pm ANNUAL

33) Keeper drop-kicks scorer

American indoor soccer never really appealed to us until we saw Brazilian keeper Sagu of the Baltimore Blast in Jackie Chan-style action. Best bits: the enormously fat ref who sends him off and the way a spotlight descends on the handbags after his insane challenge.

Search for "Sagu Baltimore Blast" or go to http://bit.ly/d4aktL

32) Physio helps Karim Benzema with his ball control

This can't be what it looks like. We hope...

Search for "La paja de Benzema" or go to http://bit.ly/cA1UcQ

65

31) High school physical

It's not just the girls who love a high school brawl. Extra points here for the punchy keeper banging his head on a wire fence after being sent off.

Search for "High school soccer/football fight" or go to http://bit.ly/aiFNBQ

CONTINUES P68

WICKED WHISTLES
CONTINUED

TV pundits ~~XXXXXXX XXXXXXX~~ and ~~XXXXXXX XXXXXXX~~ look great mates on the screen. Off it they don't speak after one took up with the other's ex.

Manager ~~XXXXXXXXXXXX~~ is famed for being one of the toughest men in the business. Wonder how his reputation would suffer if players knew he regularly puts on drag as a "surprise" at parties?

Striker ~~XXXXXXXXXXXXXXXXX~~ likes to build up an image of himself as a thoughtful type who shuns the world of bling. Then he drives off in his Bentley, which features his initials and squad number embossed in gold on the leather seats.

England star ~~XXXXXXXXXXXXXX~~ fancies himself as a gourmand. So much so that he hired legendary chef Marco Pierre White to do the catering at a dinner party – then asked the bemused cook to whip up prawn cocktail and steak.

Defender ~~XXXXXXXXXXXXXX~~ is notorious for having ideas above his station. Asked by his sponsors to attend a function at Twickenham, he demanded to be collected from his team's North London training ground – in a helicopter.

Supposedly tee-total ~~XXXXXXXXXXXXXX~~ scuppered his chances of a move to Old Trafford when United officials spotted him outside a Manchester concert hall, halfway up a lamppost and throwing traffic cones at passers-by.

Veteran administrator ~~XXXXXXXXXXXXX~~ refuses to allow his chauffeur to install SatNav in his Rolls, claiming he can direct him to any football

"It's a one-off game over two legs." – **PAUL ELLIOTT**

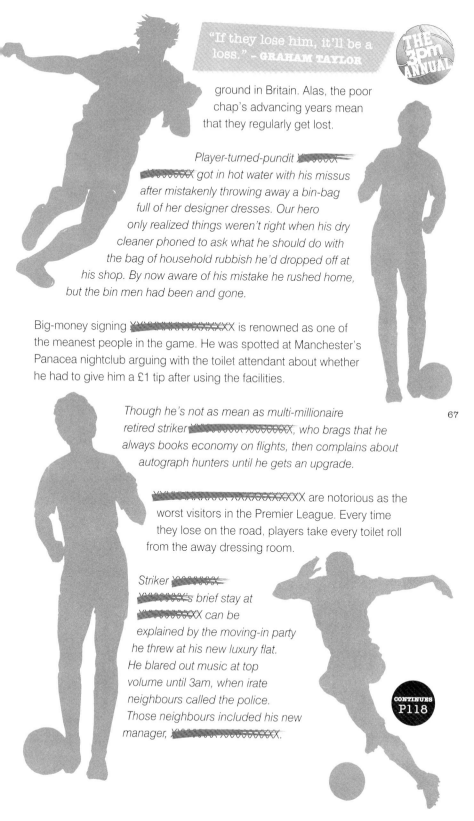

ground in Britain. Alas, the poor chap's advancing years mean that they regularly get lost.

Player-turned-pundit XXXXXX XXXXXXX got in hot water with his missus after mistakenly throwing away a bin-bag full of her designer dresses. Our hero only realized things weren't right when his dry cleaner phoned to ask what he should do with the bag of household rubbish he'd dropped off at his shop. By now aware of his mistake he rushed home, but the bin men had been and gone.

Big-money signing XXXXXXXXXXXXXXXXX is renowned as one of the meanest people in the game. He was spotted at Manchester's Panacea nightclub arguing with the toilet attendant about whether he had to give him a £1 tip after using the facilities.

Though he's not as mean as multi-millionaire retired striker XXXXXXXXXXXXXXXXX, who brags that he always books economy on flights, then complains about autograph hunters until he gets an upgrade.

XXXXXXXXXXXXXXXXXXXXX are notorious as the worst visitors in the Premier League. Every time they lose on the road, players take every toilet roll from the away dressing room.

Striker XXXXXXXXX XXXXXXXX's brief stay at XXXXXXXXXX can be explained by the moving-in party he threw at his new luxury flat. He blared out music at top volume until 3am, when irate neighbours called the police. Those neighbours included his new manager, XXXXXXXXXXXXXXXX.

67

CONTINUES P118

> *"Some players need a boot up their backside. Other players need the arm."* – **ALAN BRAZIL**

THE 50 MADDEST FOOTBALL VIDEOS... EVER
CONTINUED

30) American kid goes nuts

Poor Aiguy, as he's apparently called. The indoor soccer player has just taken a knee to the privates. Luckily, his friends are sympathetic, and stop videoing his agony after just the five minutes of traumatized testicle hilarity... but you can still hear his gonad-related groans in the background. Warning: understandably strong language.
Search for "Aiguy kneed in balls" or go to http://bit.ly/9rKSYm

29) Wind stops play

Argentina, Brazil and Spain played at Johannesburg's Ellis Park during the 2010 World Cup finals, but the most memorable football match staged there came in 2007, when Orlando Pirates faced Black Leopards. Amazingly, no one was badly injured.
Search for "Freak weather football" or go to http://bit.ly/abwWjn

28) Stadium rocks

Eintracht Frankfurt might be a mid-table Bundesliga side, but they're top of the table when it comes to supporters jumping in unison.

68

"Man City have put a spanner in the waves." – **MIKE PARRY**

Keep watching when the camera pans to some empty seats... it's doing that with good reason...
Search for "Eintracht Frankfurt fans celebrating" or go to http://bit.ly/cWe3my

27) Indonesian pitch invader goes for goal

It comes to something when your best player is a frustrated fan who runs onto the field. Here's Hendri Mulyadi's moment of near glory as he dribbles 25 yards towards the Oman net before being seen off by the friendly looking police.
Search for "Crazy Indonesia fan" or go to http://bit.ly/cKTYvE

26) Player attacks fans in Iran

69

Iran have been looking to go nuclear for years. Here, Cameroonian John Negodi does similar after his Mashhad-based side Payam Khorasan lost in their local derby against Tarbiat.
Search for "John Negodi" or go to http://bit.ly/a15tRn

CONTINUES P80

"The England game was a bit of a damp squid" – **MIKE PARRY**

THE 100 MADDEST PEOPLE IN FOOTBALL
CONTINUED

No. 60 ROBERT GREEN

England's bungling keeper is proud of his Norwich roots. He was once spotted wearing flip-flops, with his toenails painted yellow and green in a tribute to the Canaries. And he is rumoured to have spent thousands of pounds on a Warhol-style canvas of Norfolk legend Alan Partridge.

No. 59 THE VILLA PARK BRIAN SEWELLS

While working for Deadly Doug Ellis, Greasy John Gregory gave the thumbs down to Tracey Emin et al. in a sensational interview with a lads' mag, asking them: "What the f**k is art? A picture of a bottle of sour milk lying next to a smelly old jumper? What the f**k is all that about?"

Successor Martin O'Neill took up the theme recently, insisting: "I am not

into abstract art – seeing somebody put four stones together and using some bones of a dead sheep is not art."

71

No. 58 **GEORGE HARGREAVES**

When Muslim clerics in Malaysia declared that Manchester United's Red Devil logo was "un-Muslim", it must have struck a chord with George Hargreaves, leader of the Scottish Christian Party.

He has long urged a ban on the crest and said: "I urge Wayne Rooney not to honour the devil by kissing this badge. We will urge Christians to put their money elsewhere than Manchester United and its sponsors of Satanic worship."

"Repent and put The Cross of Jesus Christ or at least Star of David on your shirts. Manchester can never be UNITED under Satan. Manchester can only be UNITED under the Christian-Jewish God."

"We advise Christians in Manchester to support Manchester City, Bolton, Stockport or Burnley until the board of Manchester United change the official club symbol of Satan on all shirts, merchandise and their website."

No. 57 **DAVID JAMES**

A leading intellectual, the veteran goalkeeper once wrote that he was dissatisfied with his *Oxford English Dictionary*. "I was looking for the meaning

72

of the word 'rudimentary,' but the definition didn't satisfy me," he said. "You get a couple of lines, but you want more."

In another newspaper column, James argued convincingly that to counteract environmental disaster, clubs should pay for tree planting in Bangladesh and footballers should be encouraged to swap their Ferraris for eco-friendly hybrids. He then revealed that his latest hairstyle had been created in "a haircut shop".

No. 56 IPSWICH GREEN 'UN SUB-EDITOR

The Saturday night results paper's report of a 1-1 draw between Town and Blackpool contained a surreal interlude. See if you can spot it: "Town gained possession to see Roberts and Counago interchange passes only for the ball to run out of play for a goal kick. There was a major pigeon fanciers' convention taking place in Blackpool this week with the Tower Ballroom filled to capacity with birds and their keepers from all over the country. Garvan just failed to put Haynes through, with Walters testing the keeper before the move was cleared."

"Morten Gamst Pedersen should be given a
posthumous red card." – MIKE PARRY

No. 55 GIOVANNI TRAPATTONI

Ireland's coach still enjoys a decent relationship with the country's football journalists.

That wasn't the case during his time at Salzburg, where he once laid into the Austrian media in magnificently broken English which included these highlights: "Our training is strong. Is modern. Training wins also. I have 21 trophies. There is blah, blah, blah from you. Fools write who know nothing. Blah, blah, blah, blah. I can understand people paying. No problema. Let whistle. Is right. Have lost. But run 90 minutes! I am a professional in psychology. We train, make fitness. You people always make qua, qua, qua. S**t fools!"

No. 54 SID WADDELL

Asked to discuss "the Newcastle ethos" on Radio Five Live, the legendary darts commentator replied: "You can bring up ethos, Porthos, D'Artagnan – any of the Musketeers you like. We just want free-flowing football."

No. 53 DAVID CAMERON

England still haven't won a World Cup under a Conservative government, but that didn't stop Cameron flying a St George's flag from Downing Street during the

2010 tournament, sending good-luck messages to the squad and even watching the fateful Germany game with Angela Merkel in an attempt to appear more like one of the lads and less like an opportunist Toff who once said of his diehard support of Aston Villa: "I can only name about three players of the team I half-heartedly support and am distinctly ropey on the full details of the offside rule."

No. 52 PELÉ

As THE world's leading spokesman on erectile dysfunction, Pelé is used to talking a load of cock. But the man once memorably billed in a misspelled press release as "the immortal Pete" really steps up a gear at World Cup time. Each time the tournament rolls around, the world's greatest footballer is naturally asked for his thoughts. Alas, they tend to include statements like "Colombia will be favourites in 1994" and "an African team will have won the World Cup by the end of the 20th century," as well as the prediction that Steve McManaman ("one of the finest players in the world") would be the star of the 1998 World Cup, and

"Our target is to get into the play-offs. If not, we want automatic promotion." – GRAYS ATHLETIC'S DENNIS OLI

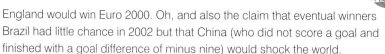

England would win Euro 2000. Oh, and also the claim that eventual winners Brazil had little chance in 2002 but that China (who did not score a goal and finished with a goal difference of minus nine) would shock the world.

In 2006 the great man excelled himself by tipping in succession Brazil, Italy, Germany, England and Japan as likely winners before telling a Mexican TV crew to expect a Mexico victory. He also told an Australian reporter that the Socceroos would beat Brazil in the group stages before the inevitable 2-0 defeat. In 2010, Pelé again went for the Mexicans but also tipped England as likely winners, with Wayne Rooney the star of the tournament.

Perhaps this is why Romario has described him as "a genius when he keeps his mouth shut" and Big Phil Scolari adds: "Pelé knows nothing about football. He has done nothing as a coach and his analysis always turns out to be wrong."

No. 51 MANCHESTER UNITED'S BACKROOM BOYS

In an attempt to defuse jokes about all United fans coming from the south,

in 2007 the club moved its marketing operation to the Mancunian suburb of London. Recent innovations from the marketing staff, meanwhile, include a £3,000 book of the club's history and a 1968 European Cup final replica shirt, in a box specially signed by Sir Bobby Charlton, for a very reasonable £395. Buyers must have been delighted to discover the gift set also bore the signature of Glazer-loving chief executive David Gill, while the shirt had a huge AIG sponsor logo on it – just like the lads of '68!

CONTINUES P82

50 GREATEST MOMENTS IN WAGDOM
CONTINUED

21) Jermaine Pennant's ex Amii Grove was asked "in waterbirds, what D is the general name for the female equivalent of a drake?" She thought it was "dragon".

22) And the late George Best's former WAG Alex blew it when asked "what V is the name for the leading wrongdoer in a play or pantomime?" She answered "Victim".

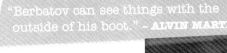

THE 3pm ANNUAL

23) In 2000, Victoria Beckham launched a solo "singing" career. David gave perhaps his most honest quote ever when he said: "I've heard Victoria's new material and it is frightening".

24) In 2005, Victoria sought to correct a Spanish journalist who quoted her as saying "I've never read a book in my life". Victoria explained she actually had never finished reading a book because of her busy schedule.

25) After Arsenal's Justin Hoyte dumped WAG Jill Demirel, she planned revenge by bedding Spurs' Tom Huddlestone. But Jill admitted: "I was praying Tom could help me get over Justin with great sex. Fat chance of that. Justin was 10 out of 10 in bed, miles better than Tom, who was a wham bam, thank you ma'am kind of guy.

When we kissed, he kept dribbling all over my mouth. I'd rate him zero out of 10." Jill first got together with Hoyte after meeting him in a jacuzzi. She held out to their third date before having sex, admitting: "I kept telling Justin it was wrong because I was engaged. But the fact we weren't supposed to made it more horny."

26) Visitors to Abbey Clancy's website are invited to buy two bookmarks of Peter Crouch's WAG in varying stages of undress for £3.49 each. But would potential buyers really own two books?

27) Carl Cort's WAG Melissa was expelled from a Tesco at Christmas 2001 when she and her husband jumped the queue, then fended off customer complaints by asking them: "Don't you know who we are?"

78

28) Amii Grove was unimpressed with ex-boyfriend Jermaine Pennant's sexual technique. She said: "He couldn't keep up with my standards in the bedroom. I'd give him a five out of 10 in bed – and that's being nice. I can understand why girls think about lesbianism." When Amii found out Jermaine had been cheating on her – by discovering another woman's panties in her bed – she locked him out of their £1.1m mansion, threw £30,000 worth of his designer clothes out of the window and smashed his Xbox.

29) Amii tried to break Pennant's video game addiction by teaching him to play board games. She said: "He became hooked on Scrabble, spending ages trying to save up the letters for the word 'zoo' – he thought it was high-scoring."

30) *WAGs Boutique* star Jadene Bircham, wife of former QPR striker Marc, signed up to a racist Facebook group called "If you don't like England then f**k off back to where you came from!" The site contained a picture of hooded Ku Klux Klan members and topics including "Hands up if you believe Enoch Powell was right", "Black ethnic groups are more likely to be criminal" and "Does Islam have anything to offer British society?" Said Jadene: "I did sign up to it but I wasn't aware that it was like that at all."

CONTINUES P114

"I love listening to games on the radio... you can't see what's going on." – ANDY TOWNSEND

THE 3pm ANNUAL

15

"We can all see that when Djibril Cissé opens his legs he's very hard to handle." – GRAHAM TAYLOR

THE 50 MADDEST FOOTBALL VIDEOS...
EVER CONTINUED

25) Best own goal ever!
Goran Rubil's body shape is perfect as he lashes home from the edge of the box. A perfect strike with just one small problem – it's in his own goal and helps Hajduk Split lose at Croatian rivals Lokomotiva.
Search for "Goran Rubil own goal" or go to http://bit.ly/bqqJnu

24) Little Britain Live!
Chesterfield's last game at Saltergate was an emotional occasion, especially when they scored late on. And one fan got a bit over-excited, much to the chagrin of his tough love-dispensing dad.
Search for "Kid in wheelchair pitch invasion" or go to http://bit.ly/bEyne5

23) Israeli celebration fail

Ever wondered whatever happened to Greasy John Gregory? The former Villa and Derby boss is currently managing Israeli strugglers Maccabi Ahi Nazrat, and while they've certainly learned how to score, full-back Mark Gorman might need to do a bit of work on his celebrations.

Search for "How not to celebrate a goal" or go to http://bit.ly/c5YKBz. See also http://bit.ly/18thXa

22) Rapping Villa granny

Pensioner Althea Gaye looks a bit like Avid Merrion in *Bo Selecta!* Yet the twist is that unlike Avid Merrion, she's doing something amusing. In this case rapping about Aston Villa's ill-fated appearance in the 2010 Carling Cup final. Best line: "Brads at the back/ Friedel and Guzan/Give it such a whack, launch a counter-attack plan". And the imaginative chorus: "Aston Veeeela, at Wembley. Playing in the final of the Carling Cup" – a stone-cold classic.

Search for "Aston Villa Carling Cup rap" or go to http://bit.ly/cXIf5t

21) Old woman gives Giggs the finger

However, Althea's not our favourite mature lady. That title is taken hands-down by this woman. We guess she's not a Manchester United fan.

Search for "Old Giggs hater" or go to http://bit.ly/bLBDbO

CONTINUES P96

THE 100 MADDEST PEOPLE IN FOOTBALL
CONTINUED

No. 50 THE PEOPLE OF STAINES

Local residents feared the worst when their non-league club drew Millwall in the FA Cup, but not everyone took matters so seriously. After the *Staines and Ashford News* reported that residents of the Wheatsheaf Lane area near the ground feared an outbreak of hooliganism, the paper's website became the target of hilarious mock-threats from Lions fans, including one advising of a Belmarsh prison "breakout by 50 hardened Millwall villains on the morning of the game. I genuinely fear for the residents of Staines."

Another correspondent, calling himself Gary Cheesefinger, wrote: "Be very careful, residents of Staines. As you know we have history and will not stop until every house in the area has had their doors knocked, and when answered our top boys will have run away.

"We will see it as a major defeat if some old girl hasn't called the Old Bill from her bungalow while 40,000 Millwall fans are urinating on her petunias."

Alas the local residents failed to spot the irony, with one posting: "I hope none of the above is true. I live in Wheatsheaf Lane and we held a community meeting on Tuesday night to voice our fears and concerns. The police seemed to play down the fear of violence, but having looked at the comments above, I'm very worried, especially as we have just bought a new car and got new windows."

No. 49 GARY COOK

Manchester City's executive chairman opened his account at Eastlands by shrugging off alleged human rights abuses by former club owner Thaksin

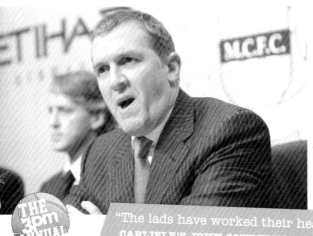

Shinawatra while describing him as "a great guy to play golf with". He then alienated defender Richard Dunne by saying that no one in Beijing had heard of him, jeopardized future superstar signings by claiming Kaka "bottled it" when

"Kitson's header was neither a cross or a shot."
— STEVE KERR, *talkSPORT*

he rejected City and enraged fans at a free club barbecue in Abu Dhabi by telling them to no longer think of the Blues as a Manchester club.

Taking to the streets of New York, he promised local City fans that they would beat United in the 2010 Carling Cup semi-finals (they lost). Undaunted, he gave a speech protesting against his bad press, and at the end of it welcomed City fan favourite Uwe Rosler "to the Manchester United hall of fame".

No. 48 STEVE McCLAREN

We're not going to lazily laugh at his famous Dutch accent here (we'll lazily laugh at it elsewhere in this book instead). But McClaren's selection policies have been in question since as early as 1985, when he named his three favourite records as Frankie Goes to Hollywood's 'Relax', Phyllis Nelson's 'Move Closer' and Meatloaf's 'Two out of Three Ain't Bad'.

"It's like the Alamo except for two things – Portsmouth don't have any bullets or arrows for their bows." — CHRIS KAMARA

84

"I can't fault Mark Palios too highly." – PAUL STURROCK

"Only time will tell if this is a point gained or three dropped." – **STEVE COPPELL**

No. 47 SIR GEOFF HURST

His 1966 heroics always guarantee him a place in hospitality at Wembley. But before one big game, Sir Geoff surprised corporate guests at a pre-match Q&A when he was asked whether he wanted Manchester United or Chelsea to win. "I couldn't give a f**k," replied the great man. "I support West Ham."

No. 46 PATRICE EVRA

He wasn't very flattering to Raymond Domenech, but the Manchester United defender knows how to lay it on with a trowel. On the day he arrived at Old Trafford, the Frenchman was assigned a club helper to show him around the city. Evra's first request was to be taken straight to church. Asked if he was religious, the defender replied he had to go to the nearest place of worship to give thanks to God for letting him join the best club in the world. Bless him.

No. 45 IAN WRIGHT

Having left the BBC complaining that he was not being taken seriously and being used as comic relief, Wrighty has since proved himself an intellectual heavyweight by hosting *Gladiators* and appearing on a chat show with Melinda Messenger. During a stint on *talkSPORT* he gave listeners a taste of his well-thought-out views on law and order: "if you get caught doing badness with guns or knives it should mean life imprisonment until they execute you".

No. 44 KEVIN NICHOLLS

"We are all in this together," wrote the then Leeds captain in his *Matchday* programme column. "It's not a case of saying it just for the sake of saying it. We believe we will pull clear."

Alas, the effect was considerably lessened by the fact that, while it was

being printed, Nicholls was stripped of the captaincy after asking for a move to Luton.

No. 43 PAT CRERAND

The former Manchester United hardman showed his legendary bias on the day Cristiano Ronaldo was sold by angrily berating a radio reporter for believing "paper talk". Until he was told the news had been broken by United's own official website. Crerand later told MUTV that "only a few hundred United fans opposed the Glazers" and surprisingly named his all-time favourite film as *The Sound of Music*: "The songs are out of this world and Julie Andrews was perfect in the lead role – it's a classic."

No. 42 ALISTAIR ROSS

Asked to comment on Ron Atkinson's racist disgrace, the eminent psychiatrist told the *Guardian*: "Big Ron's old school. We understand he comes from an era when people called a spade a spade."

No. 41 THE ARGENTINE TATTOOIST

Seeking leg action after a visit to the tattoo parlour, a fan of Boca Juniors explained: "I asked him to draw the Boca Juniors badge on my back. I didn't know he supported River Plate. I couldn't see what he was doing because he didn't have a mirror. I only found out when I got home and showed my parents that it was a tattoo of a penis."

CONTINUES
P98

"The change of wind is blowing through English football." – TONY CASCARINO

50 MADDEST WORLD CUP STORIES

The pain of summer 2010 is still fresh, but here are 50 bizarre tournament facts to cheer you up

1) American physio Jack Coll was knocked unconscious during the 1930 semi-final against Argentina when he ran onto the field to treat an injured player, dropped his bag next to the stricken Yank and was overcome by the fumes from a bottle of chloroform which had broken inside.

2) On the way home from the 2002 finals, the Senegal side stopped off for a diplomatic visit in Taiwan, where it is said players were ministered to by 37 different call girls.

3) The Senegalese also outraged locals by wearing T-shirts and flip flops for what had been advertised as a full exhibition match against the hosts. The game lasted 15 minutes.

4) Chilean coach Marco Bielsa, known as El Loco (The Madman) once gave a four-hour press conference. Bielsa also once threatened to chop off his own finger if his Argentinean club side Newell's Old Boys lost a local derby to Rosario Central.

5) Cameroon legend Roger Milla is said to have been arrested in 1992 after his plan to organize a Pygmy World Cup drew only a handful of spectators to the country's 50,000-seat Omnisports Stadium. By the third day, the disgruntled little folk, from local rain forests, were complaining about being locked in a guarded room underneath the ground with only one meal of rice and sauce in 72 hours. Said a spokesman: "You don't know the pygmies. They are extremely difficult to control. They play better if they don't eat too much."

6) Spain keeper Santiago Canizares was ruled out of the 2002 World Cup finals in May of that year, when the first-choice stopper dropped a bottle of aftershave in his hotel bathroom and a shard of glass cut the tendon in his big toe. "I do not consider myself to be unlucky by any manner of means," Canizares said.

7) A search of the crowd before the 1930 World Cup final uncovered 1,500 revolvers.

8) A book released in 2008 *(Son of the Chessmaster 2)* claims Peru's players received $50,000 per man to throw their 1978 game against Argentina, which the hosts had to win by four clear goals. The Peruvian FA is said to have received $10m, while the country also received a $100m consignment of wheat. The match finished 6-0.

9) Mwepu Ilunga, the Zaire defender who famously broke from his team's defensive wall to boot away the ball before Rivelino could take a free-kick during their 1974 finals match shouldn't have been playing in the game at all. Striker Mulumba Ndaye was sent off in the previous game against Yugoslavia for a foul committed by Mwepu. He said: "I panicked and kicked the ball away before he had taken it. Most of the Brazil players, and the crowd too, thought it was hilarious. I shouted, 'You bastards!' at them because they didn't understand the pressure we were under."

10) Heat at the 1954 game between Austria and Switzerland was so intense that one player got hyperthermia – the opposite of hypothermia – while another became disoriented and wandered off the pitch during the game, at one point being seen "defending" while standing behind his own goal.

11) Before the 2002 finals, Swedish TV aired an hour-long documentary claiming that the 1958 finals had not been held in the country but in fact had been a hoax cooked up by the American government as Cold War propaganda. Conspiracy '58 contained interviews with Swedish players of

the era admitting their matches had been stitched together from old footage – but this was itself a hoax, of course.

12) Prevented from going on the field by a FIFA official during Ireland's defeat to Mexico at USA '94, John Aldridge responded with a magnificent verbal tirade picked up by the off-field microphones. The hapless suit, clad in yellow baseball hat and light blue jacket, was told: "F*** off, you. F*** off. You t**t. You d***head. W****r. You f*****g cheat."

13) Mexico coach Ricardo Lavolpe was warned by FIFA during the 2006 World Cup after cameras caught him chain-smoking in the dugout. The former Argentine international had a magnificent tournament, calling journalists "f***ing idiots" and spending much of his time at the team's training sessions eating doughnuts under a roped-off parasol.

14) Chain-smoking coach César Luis Menotti, who led Argentina to World Cup glory in 1978, was befriended by the country's military leaders despite being a communist whose home was decorated with a framed picture of Che Guevara.

15) Brazil's legendary midfielder Socrates, who was a medical doctor despite smoking 20 cigarettes a day, was another left-winger. He listed his heroes as Che Guevara and Fidel Castro.

16) The Falkands War was still ongoing as the 1982 finals opened, and, when birds were released at the end of the opening ceremony, Irish TV commentator Jimmy Magee hailed "The symbol of peace... the pigeon."

17) Belgium's Jean Langenus reffed the 1930 Argentina v Uruguay final wearing plus fours, a tie and a deerstalker hat.

18) Italian FA chief Dr Ottorino Barassi was so worried that the German army might steal the Jules Rimet trophy that he kept it under his bed in a shoebox for the duration of the 1934 tournament.

19) BMW gave each competing team a luxury coach to use during the 1974 tournament. Police had to reclaim Zaire's after the team left their hotel in it, intending to drive it home to Africa.

20) In 2006, Ecuadorian shaman Tzamarenda Naychapi was allowed to "purify" each German stadium by letting out a loud scream to chase away evil spirits.

21) Ronaldo decided to switch to his "half-moon" hairstyle in the later stages of the 2002 tournament after he saw his infant son Ronald kissing a picture of Roberto Carlos, apparently believing the diddy defender was his dad.

22) Greeted by a Japanese hostess on arrival at the finals, Ronaldo responded by sticking out his teeth still further and making the "slitty-eyes" gesture.

23) The crowd for Romania v Peru at the 1930 finals was a whopping 300.

24) The 1974 final was delayed by 10 minutes because officials had forgotten to put in the corner and centre-line flags.

25) After Brazil paraded the Jules Rimet trophy following the 1970 final, a young supporter snatched the lid and ran. He was apprehended near the stadium exit by sub Davio.

26) Switzerland centre-forward Poldi Kielholz scored three goals in two matches at the 1934 finals despite keeping his spectacles on during matches.

27) 1938 top scorer Leonidas became a private detective after retiring.

28) Hector Castro, who scored the winner in the 1930 World Cup final, accidentally cut off his right arm with an electric saw when he was 13. He was known as El Manco (the Maimed).

29) The great Soviet keeper Lev Yashin's pre-match routine was "have a smoke to calm your nerves, then toss back a strong drink to tone your muscles".

30) Alex Villaplane, France's captain at the 1930 finals, was imprisoned in 1935 for fixing horse races and later became a gold smuggler. He joined the French Gestapo during the Nazi occupation and, after the liberation, was shot as a traitor.

31) A German newspaper sent a squad of attractive women to the Dutch team hotel before the 1974 final, leading to a story headlined "Cruyff, Champagne, Naked Girls and a Cool Bath".

92

32) Scotland wore thick wool jerseys with long sleeves and buttoned collars for their match against Uruguay at the 1954 finals. Unfortunately, the temperature was in the 30s. Midfielder Tommy Docherty said: "The Scottish FA assumed Switzerland was cold because it had mountains. The Uruguayans wore light V-necked shirts with short sleeves. We lost 7-0."

33) The string in Italy captain Peppino Meazza's shorts broke just before he took a vital penalty in the 1938 semi-final against Brazil. He took the kick while holding them up, then let them drop as he was mobbed by delighted team-mates.

34) When Juan Hohberg scored a late equalizer for Uruguay against Hungary in 1954, he was jumped on by fellow players. When they got up they discovered Hohberg had passed out.

35) The 1990 art film *Cicciolina and Moana at the World Cup* features two porn stars who sleep their way through the opposition, tiring out star performers like thinly disguised versions of Jürgen Klinsmann and Diego Maradona, thereby enabling Italy to win. The Ruud Gullit lookalike in the movie was a big lad.

36) After Scotland's disastrous start to the 1978 tournament that Ally McLeod had told supporters they would win, the manager was holding a press conference in his Cordoba hotel when a small dog ran up to him, and the manager reached down to pat the stray. "This little fellow is my last friend in the world," he said mournfully. The dog bit him.

37) Yugoslavia's Rajko Mitić failed to make the kick-off of their 1950 match against hosts Brazil in Rio because he had run into an iron girder in the players' tunnel. He emerged 20 minutes later, his head bandaged, with his team already a goal down.

38) During the 1954 "Battle of Berne" between Brazil and Hungary, English ref Arthur Ellis dismissed three players, including Joseph Bozsik, who was also a Hungarian MP. During the match a Brazilian player was struck on the head by a bottle thrown from the Hungarian bench, allegedly by legend Ferenc Puskás. Ellis later spent 18 years as the referee on BBC TV's *It's A Knockout*.

39) Garrincha, Brazil's World Cup hero of 1958 and 1962, lost his virginity at age 12. To a goat. He went on to father 14 children.

40) Not only did Diana Ross miss her penalty at the opening ceremony of USA

'94, but hostess Oprah Winfrey fell off
the stage.

41) A mugger who stole Eva
Standmann's handbag before the Brazil
v Australia game in Munich at the 2006
finals found her ticket inside and decided to enjoy the
game. Unfortunately, he sat in Eva's seat, next to her
husband Berndt, who had him arrested.

42) Romania's 1930 squad was personally selected
by King Carol II.

43) With France trailing Mexico 1-0 in their second
game of the 1930 World Cup finals, referee Almeida
Rego blew up for full-time with a French forward clear
through on goal and six minutes remaining on the clock.

44) When Brazil surprisingly lost the 1950 final to Uruguay at their own
Maracana Stadium, two fans committed suicide by jumping off a stand.
England's elimination of Cameroon in 1990 led to the suicide of a woman in
Bangladesh. Her note read: "The end of Cameroon at the World Cup means
the end of my life."

45) West Germany's Paul Breitner organized a
strike at the 1974 finals, urging his team-mates
to refuse to play unless they were guaranteed a
100,000 Deutschmark bonus each for winning the
trophy. The left-back was politically a left-winger
who was once photographed seated in a rocking
chair beneath a poster of Mao Tse-Tung, while
leafing through a Chinese communist newspaper.

46) Three key figures in the 1966 theft and recovery
of the World Cup were killed by the "Curse of
the Jules Rimet Trophy". Edward Betchley, who
supposedly stole it, died of emphysema in 1969, shortly after completing
a two-year jail term for demanding money with menaces. Joe Mears, the
FA chairman who conducted negotiations with Betchley to try to get the

trophy back, didn't even see England lift it – he died of an angina attack 10 days before the finals started. And Pickles, the mongrel who recovered it from a hedge, died in 1967.

47) Diego Maradona has admitted that during their 1-0 victory over Brazil in 1990, an Argentina player handed opponent Branco a water bottle spiked with the date-rape drug Rohypnol.

48) 2010 Brazil World Cup striker Adriano has battled a

drink problem and said of his disastrous time at Inter Milan: "I drank whatever happened to be in front of me: wine, whisky, beer... a lot of beer. I turned up every day drunk. I couldn't sleep for fear of being late but at the end I arrived in unpresentable conditions anyway and so they used to send me to sleep in the infirmary while they told journalists that I had muscle problems."

95

49) In December 2008 Napoli president Aurelio De Laurentiis warned Slovakia's Marel Hamšik off a move to Chelsea with the memorable words: "The English live badly, eat badly and their women do not wash their genitalia. To them, a bidet is a mystery."

50) In addition to being arguably the world's best goalkeeper, Italy's Gigi Buffon is undoubtedly one of football's most cerebral players. Asked in an interview, "How did you start as a goalkeeper?", he replied: "I entered my present profession by accident – a series of geographical, personal, and legal coincidences. A blend of boredom, curiosity and vanity."

THE 50 MADDEST FOOTBALL VIDEOS...
EVER CONTINUED

20) It's a gas, gas, gas

We've all seen angry players refusing to leave the field after being sent off. In Brazil, they've got a simple solution – bring on the riot police, as they did when Robson of lower league side Genus refused to walk in a match against Moto Clube in March 2010... *Search for "Brazil soccer pepper spray" or go to http://bit.ly/ c3WE9n. See also http://bit.ly/9JobAR*

96

19) When pitch invasions go bad

This shirtless Mexico fan is having a great time as he invades the pitch during a friendly with Iceland and spends 30 seconds romping around. And then it all comes to a glorious halt thanks to a security man who's clearly watched a bit of NFL in his day.
Search for "Brutal tackleada en el partido" or go to http://bit.ly/9pGbQU

18) Gerrard kid handshake

Remember the Rio Ferdinand TV specials in which the defender "merked" team-mates with a series of pranks? This is much funnier than anything Rio thought of. And it's the work of a five-year-old.

Search for "Steven Gerrard kid" or go to http://bit.ly/56odGl

17) Spot of bother

"Great, he's blown that penalty. I'll just blast it to safety..."

Search for "Impossible own goal 2008" or go to http:// bit.ly/bKB3YV

16) Head over heels hurts

Expecting a Rory Delap-style long throw into the box, the defender here goes over to block. He even protects his nether regions just in case. Alas, it's not his knackers he needs to worry about...

Search for "Funny football England throw in" or go to http://bit.ly/dsz7Zf

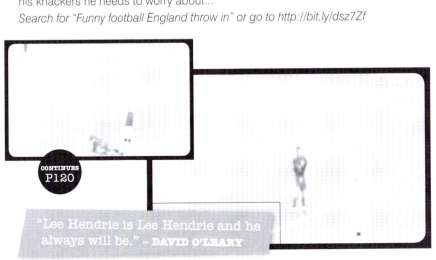

CONTINUES P120

"Lee Hendrie is Lee Hendrie and he always will be." – **DAVID O'LEARY**

THE 100 MADDEST PEOPLE IN FOOTBALL
CONTINUED

No. 40 JOHN TERRY

The deposed England skipper's off-field activities need no further discussion here. However, he deserves inclusion in our list. After news of his alleged affair with Vanessa Perroncel broke, he passed up the chance to be pictured shaking hands with Everton's matchday mascot on cancer awareness day when he realized said mascot was a giant pair of gonads known as Mr Testicles.

No. 39 DOUG ELLIS

The former Aston Villa chairman had a Stalinist taste for rebranding. He famously rechristened Villa Park's Witton Lane End the Doug Ellis Stand while the prawn sandwich brigade could relax in the Doug Ellis Boxholder Lounge.

So while we doffed our hats to generous Deadly for part-funding a new round-the-clock call-line for kids in 2009, there was little surprise among Villa fans when it was announced that it would be known as 'The Doug Ellis OBE Birmingham ChildLine Night Service'.

"Someone now has to step up and take on the mantelpiece." – RIO FERDINAND

Now the club's President Emeritus – a title he awarded himself – he stayed at Villa Park long enough for a memorable meeting with Kevin Costner, whom he hosted at a Villa game in 2004. Ellis is alleged to have repeatedly called Costner "Bob" throughout the afternoon. When a Villa Park staffer asked why, the grand old man is said to have replied: "Well, you didn't expect me to call him Mr Redford, did you?"

No. 38 **MIKE ASHLEY**

The replica shirt-wearing chairman celebrated Newcastle's first win under Kevin Keegan by flinging open the doors of the Toon directors' suite and yelling: "Let's have a party!" Soon after he advised: "Have a flutter on us climbing out of relegation trouble and into Europe". Newcastle were relegated.

"Diouf is a master of the dark art of the winger. He draws you in, he sucks you off." – **GARRY BIRTLES**

100

No. 37 SEPP BLATTER

FIFA's popular dictator was the subject of a cruel internet hoax in summer 2010, when fake additions to his Wikipedia page persuaded the South African government to award the prestigious Order of the Companions of Oliver Reginald Tambo to one 'Sepp Bellend Blatter'. Asked to comment on the story, a FIFA spokesman said he "needed to communicate the meaning of the word internally first".

Formerly President of the World Society of Friends of Suspenders, Blatter delighted feminists in 2004 by advising that attendances at women's football could be improved if the participants took to the field wearing hot pants.

"We feel unbeatable at Ewood Park – even when we play away." – DAVID BENTLEY

"Arsenal are coming forward in wave after wave of waves." – **ALVIN MARTIN**

No. 36 CAMERON JEROME

The striker's Facebook page, on which he styled himself "weezy f baby, the keys to the ladys", was a revelation. Here are Cameron's interests: "GENERAL: Chillin wiv friends, playing sports, watching mtv, going out and getting beaming! FILMS: Anything wiv densal washington in! HEROES: mum and dad, god, freinds. wiv out them i would never be where i am today! BOOKS: none yet."

No. 35 LEROY ROSENIOR

Once sacked as Torquay manager after 10 minutes when a rival consortium took over, Rosenior says his happiest times were at West Ham. He told fanzine EX: "I was in Bristol years ago when this rough-looking hard man – he was a white bloke – approached me and said: 'Are you Leroy Rosenior?' I took a step back and said: 'Yeah...'

"He gave me his card, and it had the initials I.C.F. (a reference to Hammers hooligans the Inter City Firm) on it. He told me: 'We remember you, you looked after us and if there's ever anything you want doing...

101

somebody's legs broken... then just say and we'll do it.'

"I went: 'Oh right,' and I kept that card. That fan summed it up for me – West Ham is a club that looks after its own. It's a special club."

No. 34 SIMON MILLICHIP

If the FA are seeking a man of vision to take them forward, they could do worse than contact the grandson of the former big cheese Sir Bert. The lad recently celebrated his birthday with a lavish party based on *Charlie and the Chocolate Factory*, complete with hired dwarves dressed as Oompa-Loompas. And young Simon's age? Thirty.

No. 33 DAVID BECKHAM

These days he can afford to swim in Dom Perignon, but during Manchester United's trip to Russia in 1995 Goldenballs really did bathe in bottles of Evian water after Manchester United assistant manager Brian Kidd convinced him the stuff from the tap was contaminated by fall-out from the Chernobyl disaster.

During an early interview, Beckham was asked about a programme piece in which he was described as "an accomplished artist in his spare time". He honestly confessed that he was no Picasso, but enjoyed "copying a picture of the Lion King or something like that".

His most memorable quotes include "My parents have always been there for me, ever since I was about seven" and "we want to have Brooklyn Christened but we're not sure what religion yet".

No. 32 RICHARD BUTLER

When Notts County's coach stopped at a petrol station, the midfielder spotted a sign instructing drivers not to use mobile phones on the forecourt and enquired of a team-mate: "Is it to stop people dropping their phones down the petrol cap?"

No. 31 MONTY AND RUPERT

The Emirates is a rough old place. With notorious hardmen Melvyn Bragg and Geoffrey Palmer in the stands and Raymond Blanc dishing up the half-time pies in the Diamond Club, it's a proper naughty throwback to the bad old days of English football. Well, not really. And nothing sums that up better than the magnificent stadium announcement heard there in February 2010: "Could Monty and Rupert please report to the nearest steward?" The away fans laughed all the way home to Sunderland...

102

CONTINUE P122

"Sly Stallone will be at Everton promoting his new film, Rocky Bilbao." – **ALAN BRAZIL**

"When Jason Koumas is on form, he's the type of player who calls all the strings." – **IAN RUSH**

THREE LIONS, 50 WEIRD FACTS

We might not have troubled the trophy cabinet since '66, but England can still amaze...

1) Segar Bastard won one England cap, in a 5-4 defeat to Scotland in 1880. Brilliantly, he was also a referee.

2) The original title of England/New Order's 1990 No. 1 'World In Motion' was 'E for England' – but even the FA could see through the thinly veiled drug reference.

104

3) Tunisian referee Ali Bin Nasser, who gave Diego Maradona's Hand of God goal, claimed his eyesight had been affected by medicine he was taking to cure his piles problem.

THE 3pm ANNUAL

4) Jeff Astle was accused of being drunk when he had to be helped off England's 1970 flight to Mexico. The team doctor blamed air sickness and Astle said the rumours were "scandalous".

5) After a dog strayed on the pitch during the 1962 England v Brazil match and urinated on Jimmy Greaves, Garrincha adopted it and took it home.

6) Emile Heskey's middle name is Ivanhoe, while Ledley King's is Brenton. Gary Lineker's is Winston and Bobby Moore's was Chelsea.

105

7) Alf Ramsey's childhood home did not have running water, electricity or an inside lavatory.

8) A 1970 album by the England squad, titled *The World Beaters Sing The World Beaters*, contained a version of 'Sugar Sugar' sung by Bobby Moore and Francis Lee.

9) During the 2006 World Cup campaign, English journalists played "Sven Bingo" during the coach's press conferences, ticking off clichés like "first half good, second half not so good" and "Wine Roney" as they were uttered by manager Sven-Göran Eriksson.

"Spurs fans are feeling very boyish about the future." – **ALAN BRAZIL**

10) When Sir Bobby Robson did a mammoth signing session for one of his many autobiographies, the chap at the back of the queue finally handed over his book and remarked, "You've signed a few of these today, eh?" "Hundreds son, hundreds," came the weary reply. When the buyer got his book home later, he discovered it was signed "Best wishes, Bobby Hundreds".

11) In a doomed attempt to be fit for the 1990 World Cup, Bryan Robson flew 70-year-old faith healer Olga Stringfellow to Italy to treat his Achilles injury. Robson also tried the services of Glenn Hoddle's favourite Eileen Drewery, of whom manager Bobby Robson said: "He put her hands over Bryan's leg and blue sparks flew out of her fingers. Robbo jumped off the table and we both said: 'F***ing hell'."

12) Glenn Hoddle chose a CD by American soft-jazz saxman Kenny G as the perfect background music to score him dumping players including Paul Gascoigne from his 1998 finals squad. It worked so well Gazza only destroyed a lamp and a table in his fury. Hoddle was spotted at one of the G-Man's gigs in London during 2009.

In 2010, Hoddle attempted to deny the G-man in a manner not seen since St Peter turned his back on Christ. He wrote: "Since that day when I finalised the squad, it has been written that Kenny G was playing in my room when I told the players the bad news. Where does this nonsense come from?"

Alas, the nonsense came from Hoddle himself, who wrote in his book, 'My 1998 World Cup Story': "I'd made a mental note to bring a selection of CDs with me and had Kenny G playing in the background because I felt that some of the players might be a bit nervous walking into a silent room."

13) When journalists arrived at Alf Ramsey's house for quotes on the day after the 1966 World Cup final, they were told: "Go away. Today is my day orf."

14) Ramsey attempted to hide his Dagenham accent and is claimed to have taken elocution lessons – though he always denied it. His attempts to sound posh sometimes backfired, as when he was asked how long a floodlight failure would delay kick-off and replied: "Ay em not an helectrician."

15) Neil Webb, who played for England in the 1990 third place play-off match, became a postman after his football career faltered and is now a forklift truck driver.

16) With players of the same name from Everton and Spurs making Bobby Robson's squad, England fans at the 1986 World Cup used the tune of 'Guantanamera' to sing "Two Gary Stevens, There's Only Two Gary Stevens".

107

17) England's 1982 World Cup song 'This Time (We'll Get It Right)' was co-written by Chris Norman and Pete Spencer of 'Living Next Door To Alice' hitmakers Smokie. They also wrote Kevin Keegan's hit 'Head Over Heels In Love'.

18) Ivor Broadis, who played for England at the 1954 finals, has lived in the same Carlisle semi for the last 55 years.

19) Walter Winterbottom was England's manager at four World Cups but was not allowed to pick the team. Those duties were handled by a panel of selectors. One, a fish merchant from Grimsby named Arthur Drewry, refused to select Stanley Matthews in the ill-fated game against the USA in 1950 because he had missed the previous victory against Chile.

"The money footballers earn today is incredulous." – BOBBY GOULD

20) While an England player, Bobby Robson was often critical of team-mate George Cohen's wayward shooting. He said: "George has hit more photographers than Frank Sinatra". Robson also said of his England playing career: "Denis Law once kicked me at Wembley in front of the Queen in an international. I mean, no man is entitled to do that really."

21) When organizers of Italia 90s TV coverage had the splendid idea of augmenting team line-ups with film of each player mouthing his own name, Paul Gascoigne subverted the process by silently saying "f***ing w***ker". It was screened by the BBC and ITV all the way through the tournament.

22) England squad member Ian Callaghan was given a special responsibility at the 1966 final. Nobby Stiles handed him his dentures in an envelope and said: "If we win the Cup, Cally, for goodness sake get them back to me so I've got them in for the photo shoots." Alas, the Liverpool man couldn't get on the pitch because of security and a gap-toothed dancing legend was born.

108

23) Boy of '66, Ray Wilson was born in Shirebrook, Derbyshire, but his mother had to go to Mansfield to register his birth because the local registrar refused to record his first name as Ramon, after Mexican silent movie star Ramon Navarro.

24) After losing his place to Terry Cooper, Wilson retired from international football before the 1970 finals and bought an undertaker's business in Huddersfield, which he ran for nearly 30 years before retiring in 1997.

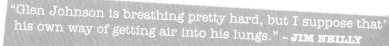

"Glen Johnson is breathing pretty hard, but I suppose that's his own way of getting air into his lungs." – **JIM NEILLY**

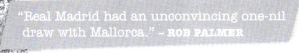

THE 3pm ANNUAL

25) Asked what he would be were he not a footballer, Peter Crouch replied, "a virgin". In August 2010, Crouch was revealed to have cheated on lovely fiancee Abbey Clancy with a prostitute named Monika Mint, who handily produced a receipt reading 'Monika, Prostitute, 100 Euros'. Said Ms Mint: "Although he's not good looking, Peter was very friendly and was gentle with me the whole time. In spite of the langauage barrier he was very intimate and touched me nicely."

26) England keeper David James collects Raleigh Chopper bikes.

27) Former England captain Emlyn Hughes named his children Emlyn Jnr and Emma Lynn. Though Emlyn's official nickname was "Crazy Horse", ex-Liverpool team-mate Tommy Smith called him "Thrush" as "he was an irritating c***".

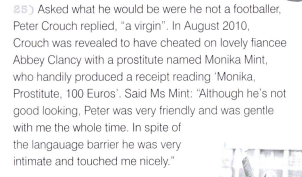

109

28) Before one England tournament, Bobby Robson told Tony Adams not to kick the ball downfield as "it will go straight to Maradona and he'll come back at us". Players sensibly pointed out that since this was the 1988 European Championship finals, the cheating Argentine would not be involved.

29) Peter Shilton was rescued by police in September 1980 after an irate husband found Shilts "parked" with his wife on a dirt track behind Nottingham racecourse. He called the cops when the keeper bravely refused to open the doors of his Jaguar.

30) Brian Labone pulled out of England's 1966 World Cup squad because he was getting married that summer. The marriage was later dissolved. Labone also attempted to retire before the 1970 finals – which he ended up playing in – because he wanted to take over his dad's central heating business.

31) Between matches at the 1990 finals, crazy guys Chris Woods and Terry Butcher went to a Cagliari restaurant with their tracksuits turned inside out and proceeded to eat a meal in reverse order – coffee, dessert, main course and the starter last.

32) Bill McGarry, who played for England at the 1954 World Cup finals, enraged Wolves players during his managerial career by banning prawn cocktails from their pre-match meals.

33) During the 1998 finals, England players attempted to alleviate the boredom of TV interviews by sneaking song titles into their answers. Gareth Southgate was first to score, being asked what he thought of the team hotel and replying: "It's hardly Club Tropicana". Then pressed by Bob Wilson on what the team would be for the first match, he said: "You won't be getting any Careless Whispers from me, Bob."

34) Tony Adams set a cracking pace by opening his first interview of the tournament with the words: "I'm So Excited. There have been some Magic Moments this season", before shoehorning four Beatles' songs – 'Get Back', 'Something', 'Let It Be' and 'With A Little Help From My Friends' – into a subsequent chat.

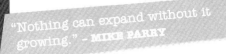

35) Alas, Alan Shearer blew the gaff by unwittingly using the phrase "against all odds" and punching the air when he realized it was also the title of a Phil Collins song. Talk of the stunt spread, so much that Shearer was later asked whether it was actually going on, and replied: "It's Just Your Imagination". Finally, with TV demanding to know if the prank was still ongoing, he said: "No. It's All Over Now."

36) When England went on a pre-World Cup tour of Mexico in 1969, Alf Ramsey held a press conference to soften up the locals. Asked if he had a message for the Mexican people, he replied: "Yes. There was a band playin' outside our hotel at five this mornin'. We were promised a motorcycle escort to the ground. It never arrived. When our players went out to inspect the pitch, they were abused and jeered. I would have thought the Mexican public would have been delighted to welcome England. But we are delighted to be in Mexico and the Mexican people are a wonderful people."

111

37) 1970 World Cup striker Jeff Astle later worked as a window cleaner and had a sign saying: "He misses no corners".

38) Peter Shilton and Gary "Honest Links" Lineker were the bookies at England race nights during the 1990 World Cup, in which players would bet on pre-recorded races. Having lost heavily, Paul Gascoigne persuaded physio Fred Street to acquire one of the tapes and instructed everyone to pile on a rank outsider in the final race at the last minute. Unsurprisingly, the

horse came in and cost Lineker and Shilton thousands.

39) After Goldenballs' dismissal in the 1998 World Cup, a billboard in front of a Baptist church in Mansfield read: "God Forgives Even David Beckham."

40) The final foul tally in the notorious "animals" match during the 1966 finals was 33 committed by England and 19 committed by Argentina. However, the Argentines made up for it with a post-defeat near-riot in which players urinated on their dressing room wall, covered a FIFA official's blazer in spittle, tried to tear off referee Rudolf Kreitlein's jacket and attempted to break into the England dressing room for a fight. Kreitlein retired after the game.

112

41) Before playing Portugal in the 2006 quarter-finals, Wayne Rooney was asked by Garth Crooks: "Is it a day for cool heads, Wayne?" He replied: "Yes, we know not to get involved" – and was promptly dismissed for stamping on Ricardo Carvalho's testicles.

42) When Geoff Hurst's third goal went in at the end of the 1966 final and England trainer Harold Shepherdson jumped up and down with the rest of the bench, Alf Ramsey said: "Sit down Harold, I can't see."

43) Rodney Marsh's international career was ended by Alf Ramsey after England's manager instructed him to pull his socks up or risk being pulled off at half-time. Marsh responded: "Crikey, we only get an orange at Man City."

44) Sir Bobby Robson once remarked that "we don't want our players to be monks, we want them to be football players because a monk doesn't play football at this level." Asked in 1990 whether he had underestimated quarter-final opponents Cameroon, he replied: "We didn't underestimate them. They were just a lot better than we thought."

45) 1966 hero Alan Ball once confessed that when he reached his seventies he would like to "die for his country in a foreign field". Alas, Bally died of a heart attack while putting out a bonfire at home in 2006, aged 61.

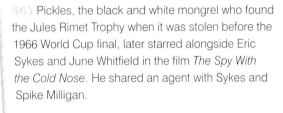

46) Pickles, the black and white mongrel who found the Jules Rimet Trophy when it was stolen before the 1966 World Cup final, later starred alongside Eric Sykes and June Whitfield in the film *The Spy With the Cold Nose*. He shared an agent with Sykes and Spike Milligan.

47) Unfortunately, Pickles didn't live long enough to enjoy the fame. He accidentally hung himself a year later while chasing a cat, catching his choker lead on the branch of a tree and going undiscovered for more than an hour.

113

48) The *New York Times* refused to report that the USA had beaten England 1-0 at the 1950 World Cup because editors believed the scoreline was a hoax.

49) Future England caretaker manager Howard Wilkinson once berated the Leeds United press corps with the words: "What do you lot know anyway? How many caps have you won?" Former England captain Jimmy Armfield, there with Radio Five Live, replied: "Forty-three, Howard." Armfield later told listeners: "There's a real international flavour to this World Cup."

50) Graham Taylor, turned into a national laughing stock after the infamous "Impossible Job" TV documentary once observed: "Very few of us have any idea whatsoever of what life is like living in a goldfish bowl – except, of course, for those of us who are goldfish."

50 GREATEST MOMENTS IN WAGDOM
CONTINUED

31) Nigel Quashie's former WAG Suzanne Franklin exited their relationship with a £1,800 Gucci Hysteria handbag, a £1,240 Louis Vuitton Mahina Denim XL handbag, a £975 Jimmy Choo Riki handbag, a £924 Chloe Paddington handbag, a £800 Prada Dip Dye Purse, a £425 Louis Vuitton Musette Salsa handbag and a £400 Coccinelle handbag. She said: "I told him I'd rather spend £50 on a bag from Topshop."

32) *I'm A Celebrity*... veteran Nicola McLean, WAG of Bristol City's Tom Williams, explained she had to have breast implants as "my own were quite nice really, but I was never happy with them. Like most girls', they'd fluctuate depending on the time of the month. I'd show up to a topless photoshoot, get my kit off and I'd never know if they'd be big and bouncy or a bit on the disappointing side. It was doing my head in."

114

33) Coleen Rooney is said to spend £20,000 in Liverpool boutique Cricket each season. Cricket owner Justine Mills' Bebo website includes this biography: "hello i am justine i own the shop cricket in liverpool it has been open for 14 years an has made a name for it self with the WAGS walking around with cricket

"He's the headstone of English football." – GRAHAM BEECROFT

"The game is in a neutral country, for both teams." – **DAVID BECKHAM**

bags of there arms. cricket is mostly wore by footballers from liverpool an everton an wags but non famous people shop here to... we have are fantastic models for cricket which get there pictures took in the

new clothes... if you can not get down to liverpool to by are wounderfull things why not get stuff of are website. thank you justine x".

34) Vanessa Perroncel appeared in a 2004 film adaptation of *Phantom of the Opera*, billed as a "candelabra holder".

35) Coleen Rooney has released three fragrances – Coleen, Coleen Summer and Coleen Black. All are available at Superdrug.

"Paul Scholes is literally on another planet." – **KIERON DYER**

36) In 2007 Alex Curran released her own fragrance, cleverly titled Alex.

37) After Jamie O'Hara ditched lover of four years Sade Metcalfe for uberWAG Danielle Lloyd, he cushioned the blow by taking back the £28,000 silver Mercedes SLK he'd given Sade for Christmas.

38) Charlotte Mears was hired by the Foreign Office to give advice to young women about the perils of going abroad. Her tips included "it might sound trivial, but you never know when you might break a nail or your extensions turn green in the pool... Get a number of good local beauticians or check if the hotel has one before you go!" She added a reminder to buy travel

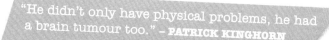

"He didn't only have physical problems, he had a brain tumour too." – PATRICK KINGHORN

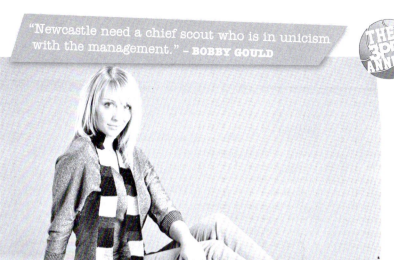

insurance before flying: "One tumble off a bar table in your Jimmy Choos could cost you £20,000 worth of shopping money on your hospital bill!"

39) Steve Sidwell's wife Krystell says her favourite restaurant is the "lovely" Suka because "they bring Thai dishes to you at different stages". Sidwell has their 100-word wedding vows tattooed on his back. They include this passage: "From day one you've been the rock by my side, the driving force behind me. You give me my strength and my confidence. You make me smile and happy every day that I'm with you."

40) Joe Cole's WAG Carly Zucker had to give up her day job because of the intolerable strain of juggling that with living at their Surrey mansion. She said: "I tried it before with the personal training as well as running the house, and it just made me stressed and unhappy."

CONTINUES P130

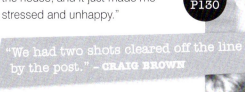

WICKED WHISTLES
CONTINUED

Midlands hard man ~~XXXXXXXXXXXXXXXX~~ is renowned for his punishing training regime. He picked out a dog from a pet rescue home and took it along on one of his gruelling runs – and it promptly keeled over and died.

Striker ~~XXXXXXXXXXXXXXX~~ complained to his manager that team-mates were freezing him out. They had to tell the gaffer it was because they'd spotted him out clubbing while wearing a pink Stetson.

Midfielder ~~XXXXXXXXXXXXXXXXXX~~ couldn't be bothered getting out of his car to watch his brother play parks football. Instead he drove his tricked-out Range Rover across several Sunday League pitches – many occupied – so he could get a close-up view of the action.

England fringe player ~~XXXXXXXXXXXXXXX~~ is dismissively known to his club's coaching staff as "Charles Atlas". It's because of his "accidental" habit of frequently pulling up his shirt during matches to reveal his magnificently toned six-pack to an otherwise unimpressed crowd.

Weirdo ~~XXXXXXXXXXXXXXXX~~'s party piece is revolting. He invites a mate to wee into his cupped hands... then washes his face with it.

Mild-mannered manager ~~XXXXXXXXXXXXXX~~ took his dismissal from Premier League ~~XXXXXXXXXXXXXX~~ well. He literally emptied his office after getting his P45, his spoils including a box of PG Tips and a doorstop.

Midfielder and self-styled ladies' man ~~XXXXXXXXX~~ ~~XXXXXXXXX~~ is famed for his pre-season ritual of demanding special sets of specially tailored shorts from the kit

THE 3pm ANNUAL

manufacturer – which he thinks will accentuate the size of his package.

Premier League starlet ▨▨▨▨▨▨▨▨ refused to play in a reserve match because he told his manager he "had plans" for the evening. "What will happen if I don't play?" asked the player. "You'll get fined two weeks' wages," said his boss. "OK," said the young upstart – and he wrote out a cheque for £42,000.

Swarthy foreigner ▨▨▨▨▨▨▨▨ is famous for wearing a headband. It's not a fashion thing – it keeps his long-haired wig in place.

Premier League newcomer ▨▨▨▨▨▨▨▨ spent only 10 minutes in the Canary Wharf flat his London club bought him as a signing-on present. He phoned them from the car park to say the deal was off unless he got one with river views instead.

"Martin Jol is literally a dead man walking." – **STEVE CLARIDGE**

THE 50 MADDEST FOOTBALL VIDEOS... EVER
CONTINUED

15) Marc Bircham and the snake

You've probably had enough of tedious football anecdotes after reading this book. But this one, from QPR veteran Marc Bircham, is worth sticking around for. It involves a kit man, a hotel room, a python and the delicate art of "giving a snake options".
Search for "Marc Bircham snake" or go to http://bit.ly/a95c4K

14) Best penalty ever

Over 9 million YouTubers have viewed this clip. But it doesn't get any less funny.
Search for "Penalty in face" or go to http://bit.ly/M3jze

13) The brawl to end them all

Pre-season games don't get any less friendly than this clash between Chinese side Beijing Guoan and Pohang Steelers of North Korea. Players, subs in bubble jackets, coaches, kit men and passers-by all get involved. Our favourite is the bloke who brings along a folded chair.
Search for "Beijing Guoan Pohang Steelers" or go to http://bit.ly/a3G90C

120

12) **"You can bring your dinner"**

It's now over 15 years since doomed Leyton Orient manager John Sitton delivered a blistering on-camera half-time team talk to his players after they fell behind at home to Blackpool. Immortalized on the TV documentary *Club for a Fiver*, the deranged gaffer tells all his players they're going to get made redundant, sacks full-back (and his mate) Terry Howard and then picks a fight with two other players, issuing the immortal threat: "You can pair up if you like, and you can f***ing pick someone else to help you, and you can bring your f***ing dinner." Sitton is now a taxi driver.

Search for "Sitton bring your dinner" or go to http://bit.ly/zbQ9U

121

11) **Coleen Rooney "parking"**

Housewife, mother, celeb mag journalist, Superdrug fragrance designer Mrs Wayne is a woman of many talents. But sticking her Ferrari between two

white lines isn't one of them.

Search for "Coleen Rooney arriving in Ferrari" or go to http://bit.ly/aC205D

CONTINUES P132

"We've ended the season on a high – apart from the last game, which we lost." – **DAVID BECKHAM**

THE 100 MADDEST PEOPLE IN FOOTBALL
CONTINUED

No. 30 PAUL MERSON

The former Arsenal midfielder, who once admitted he had become interested in cocaine because it ensured he could drink 10 pints a night rather than the usual seven, has forged post-football careers in after-dinner speaking, professional gambling and punditry, all with mixed results. His betting went awry to such an extent he was forced to move back home to his parents at the age of 40. A speech in a Watford pub misfired when Merse's brave opening line – "ask me anything you like, no boundaries" – was greeted with the response: "Who's your dealer?" The expert predictions, meanwhile, looked good when Merson correctly called last year's FA Cup semi, telling Chelsea TV: "A few weeks ago the FA Cup semi would have been heads

"Craig Beattie's quick, he's very fast, and he's got great pace." – **ALEX McLEISH**

or tails, but after the 7-1 win I can only see one winner – Chelsea. I'll go for 3-0." Unfortunately it was then discovered that a day earlier he had told the *Birmingham Mail*: "Villa have the team to beat them in my opinion. I was a big Chelsea fan when I was a kid but I do fancy Aston Villa in this one."

Merson played a huge part in Portsmouth's 2005 promotion, but begged Harry Redknapp for a mid-season week off in order to tackle his gambling and drink problems at Tony Adams' Sporting Chance clinic. Redknapp agreed, and was delighted to get a phone call from a friend a few days later, telling him he'd just seen Merse looking in rude health. "Paul's in great form," said the pal. "We've just had a few beers together on the beach in Barbados."

123

No. 29 **LEE BOWYER**

Birmingham's – ahem – combative midfielder is good with numbers. When Carson Yeung took over the club, one of the club's new Hong Kong advisers asked Bowyer to imagine the scope for the club if they could win over the Chinese market, asking whether he knew just how many people lived in the country. Lee went for 22 million… a mere 1,578,000,000 people short.

No. 28 **MRS WES BROWN**

Three months before their wedding in July 2009, the Manchester United

Orangeman's fiancée Leanne Wassell told local paper the *Wilmslow Express* that she "wasn't even thinking about selling the rights to a glossy magazine. You can go two ways when you start going out with a footballer. But I never really wanted to be in the limelight."

Leanne then dodged the limelight by appearing across eight pages of *OK!* magazine, which revealed that the defender wore a £400 pair of shoes made from the skin of a stingray while his missus opted for "a specially made pair of Christian Louboutin shoes that took several trips to Paris to perfect. The date of the wedding was spelled out on the back of the heels in Swarovski crystals."

No. 27 BRYAN GUNN

The Dr Bunsen Honeydew lookalike was in confident mood before the big kick-off of August 2009, telling his local paper: "The fact that we're unbeaten during pre-season builds our confidence. The new signings have come in with a winning mentality. Every time they wear the shirt they want to do well, not only for themselves but for the supporters too. That's why I expect our players to go out and achieve a winning result." The headline was "City peaking at the right time, says Gunn".

A day later, his Norwich City side opened the season in style, losing 7-1 at home to Colchester – Gunn was fired.

No. 26 THE REVEREND SUN MYUNG MOON

Aston Villa picked up a nice trophy and £1.2millon in prize money by winning the 2009 pre-season Peace Cup. Unfortunately, they had to collect both prizes from the Revd, an ex-jailbird, retired arms manufacturer, mass wedding planner and right-wing basher of gays as "dung-eating dogs". The oddball cult leader who in 2004 hired a Washington government building to stage a bizarre coronation in which he declared himself "humanity's saviour, messiah, returning lord and true parent", handed the trophy to Villa's then skipper Nigel Reo-Coker, but it's unlikely they discussed the 1974 speech on race in which Moon is said to have claimed of the world that "Orientals can contribute in the spiritual aspect, white people can contribute in the analytical, scientific area, while black people can contribute in the physical area – physical educational development of physical fitness, the area of health. The talented area of black people is in this physical aspect."

No. 25 STEVE BULL

Part of the striker's art is heading the ball. Wolves' legendary striker might have headed a few too many. Asked in late 2009 who his dream dinner guest would be, Bully opted for "Muhammad Ali – if he was still alive."

125

No. 24 RIO FERDINAND

The only England player who emerged from the 2010 World Cup with credit, Ferdinand has long been praised for his timing and anticipation. This might explain why, in last summer's issue of the bmi baby in-flight magazine, Rio could be found extolling the virtues of Manchester eaterie Rosso, saying: "The vibe is nice and relaxed, with a casual dress code which I like. Plenty of footballers pop in for some quality food after matches and not just United

126

players either. The chef is as hot as mustard! I love the flattened steak if I'm having a big main or the penne pasta, which is so good it's ridiculous." At the time, Rosso was still two months away from penning its doors for the first time, a fact which eluded its proprietor, Mr Rio Ferdinand. Rio later launched the commendable *5 Magazine*, whose third issue contained an illustrated guide to tying a scarf. It read: "1: Place scarf over neck with one end hanging longer than the other. 2: Pull the longer end around your neck and bring to the front. 3: Loop one end over the other and adjust for comfort."

"I'd love the person who taught José Mourinho English to taught me." – **STEVE CLARIDGE**

> "It wasn't only the manner Arsenal got beat, it
> was the way they got beat." – **WARREN BARTON**

No. 23 **FREDDY EASTWOOD**

Fined in 2009 for fly-tipping rubbish including bank statements with his name on them, Eastwood is a favourite opponent in football card schools. Former team-mate Graham Stack revealed: "When it's blackjack, Freddy never knows when he's got 21. I tell him he's bust, and he declares."

No. 22 **CHLOE EVERTON**

Not since the glory days of Saucy Sid and Busty Babs had we seen double entendres the size of the massive ones served up by Sky Sports newsreader Chloe on her Twitter page. They included: "Delap using a towel to mop up some of the wet, ready for those long thrusting balls into the box"; "Sat in a restaurant in Shepherds Bush, and the owner just asked me if I wanted to sample his juices"; "Kovac's big tackle is going to get red if he isn't careful"; "the sign on the ticket machine says: slot out of action. I know the feeling"; and "it's Sunday so I am definitely up for a roast".

During the cold winter she excelled herself with "slipped over on the ice, luckily I've only got a small gash" and "So much snow. On days like this it's slushy round the front so best to enter via the back door" before being told to stop by spoilsport Sky bosses.

127

No. 21 **MARTIN JOL**

The Dutch Fungus the Bogeyman lookalike ducked a Premier League return with Fulham in summer 2010, possibly to circumvent further British press sniggers about his siblings' names. While at Spurs, Jol memorably ranted: "It's stupid. My brother has to go around and introduce himself as Cornelius to everyone now. Cock is just a nickname in Holland, a short version of his name. This is normal in Holland. It's his name and my other brother's name is Dick. I mean, what's so funny about that?"

CONTINUES P134

PARTY TIME
WITH RIO

Rio Ferdinand is a notorious celebration-crasher, often running the length of the field to ~~make sure he gets on all the photographs~~ salute his successful team-mates. And, judging by these exclusive photos, it's been going on longer than you'd think...

"Sir Alex Ferguson IS Manchester United. If you cut him, he bleeds red." – **ALAN BRAZIL**

"Sometimes you have to swallow the unswallowable." – **ARSENE WENGER**

50 GREATEST MOMENTS IN WAGDOM
CONTINUED

41) When Emile Heskey's WAG Chantelle Tagoe appeared on *Celebrity Come Dine With Me*, she was asked about the huge picture of Martin Luther King on her dining room wall. She admitted: "I'm not sure who he is... anyway, look at my lovely cutlery!"

42) Chantelle later warned her guests that their potatoes might be a bit hard as she'd never boiled spuds in her life.

43) On the same programme, Jessica Lawlor declared her preference for "Thigh green curry".

130

44) And Nicola T asked what was in a papaya salad.

45) Jessica's plans to macerate raspberries in expensive liqueur went awry when she forgot to take the fruit out of the punnet. So the booze merely ran through the holes in the bottom.

46) Vanessa Perroncel – who denies sleeping with John Terry – says she dreams about blowing up the offices of the *News Of The World*. In her fantasy, according to Vanessa, she is wearing a hard hat and grinning cheesily for photographers as she plunges the detonator's handle.

47) Alex Curran has described as "just silly" rumours that she had botox injected into her 15,000 Hermes handbag to keep it looking fresh.

"I don't want to sound homophobic, but I want a Scottish manager." – PAT NEVIN

48) When Abbey Clancy told him she never got less than a B grade in any school examination, Peter Crouch demanded to see her GCSE certificate.

49) When Emile Heskey's WAG Chantelle Tagoe visited poverty-stricken kids at the Baphumelele Children's Home near Cape Town, during the 2010 World Cup, she did so wearing a white trouser suit teamed with a £350 Chanel belt.

50) As a teenager, Gary Lineker's wife Danielle Bux narrowly avoided injury when a shellsuit she was wearing melted in front of her family's coal fire.

131

THE 50 MADDEST FOOTBALL VIDEOS... EVER CONTINUED

10) Worst ghost goal ever

Everyone's seen the bizarre Reading goal at Watford, given despite crossing the touchline a good two yards wide of the goal. But this one from Germany, awarded to FC Duisburg in a match against FSV Frankfurt, is just as logic-defying.

Search for "Phantomtor Tiffert" or go to http://bit.ly/b4tEib. See also http://bit.ly/14HCR0

132

9) Steve McClaren speaks Dutch

Yes, you've seen it so many times before. But did people boo when Frank Sinatra sang 'My Way' for the 93,648th time? Best bits? "Liverpool or Arsenal, I thought maybe one of them we would draw, and it is Arsenal, I think." And the magical way he struggles for words in his own native language as he says: "I say, erm, I think we are not just, what you call, underdogs, we are masshive underdogs."

Search for "Steve McClaren goes Dutch" or go to http://bit.ly/4C7Bch

8) Female reporter meets player close up

Pitchside reporting is a dangerous

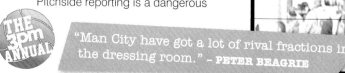

"Man City have got a lot of rival fractions in the dressing room." – **PETER BEAGRIE**

business. But while anyone colliding with Sky's Nick Collins would simply bounce off his enormous moustache, this Spanish journo isn't so lucky.

Search for "Soccer match reporter fail" or go to http://bit.ly/cdkBwV

7) Happy Evra After

Now this is truly bizarre. It's Patrice Evra, before his Manchester United days, appearing to do a Chris Tucker impression while saying incredibly rude things about Jimmy Floyd Hasselbaink, Frank Lampard and a cat. You've

got to watch this. Warning: strong language.
Search for "Patrice Evra high pitched voice" or go to http://bit.ly/F0KYq

6) Gary Neville prank call

More strong language here as the

133

Old Trafford Chuckle Brother tears a strip off a youngster who's acquired his phone number from a school-mate. As becomes apparent, quite a few of the lads' mates appear to have been phoning Gary and disturbing him from his normal duties of burning Beatles records, throwing darts at pictures of Stan Boardman and shouting whenever John Bishop comes on the telly.

Search for "Gary Neville phone call" or go to http://bit.ly/bbp1ee

CONTINUES P146

THE 100 MADDEST PEOPLE IN FOOTBALL
CONTINUED

No. 20 ROY KEANE

So eager is Keane not to trade on his past glories that since leaving Old Trafford he refuses to sign anything Manchester United-related. This led to a splendid incident when he declined to inscribe a fan's book, on the grounds that it was linked to the Red Devils. The book was Keane's own autobiography.

Keane's refusal to suffer fools gladly is as famous as his dog-walking skills. It's been said that he once tore a strip off Ruud van Nistelrooy after he saw the Dutchman preparing for a TV interview by combing his hair, and that Roy singled out Darren Fletcher for abuse when he saw the young Scot playing with a Gameboy. Best of all was Keane's reaction when Gary Neville changed his mobile phone number. The defender texted friends and colleagues with the number and the message "This is Gary Neville's new phone number". Minutes later, a text reply came back from Keane. It read "So what?"

Yet he will be best remembered for the Vesuvian temper which saw him tell Mick McCarthy to "stick it up your bollocks" in Saipan and, more recently, ask for a tactics whiteboard to be brought into the Sunderland dressing room at half-time simply so he could kick it over.

In 2010 he impressed at an Ipswich press conference when a polite request about possible interest in Celtic's Stephen McManus was greeted with a tirade that included "total rubbish", "absolute disgrace" and "bloody lies".

Matters then escalated, with Keane telling the journo: "You're bloody disgraceful. Blatant lies. You want my respect? You bloody earn it. Same as I have to earn the respect of the Ipswich fans."

He added: "Speak to your sources. Whoever your bloody sources are. You must have a source, obviously? Absolute disgrace you are."

After Town's press officer hastily announced, "Thank you gentlemen, that will be all", Keane stood a couple of paces away from his adversary's face and called him a "f***ing liar" before storming out.

No. 19 MICHAEL OWEN

The ageing wonderboy has admitted his dislike for anything fictional, preferring to watch sporting events, the news or documentaries (but mainly sporting events).

By the time he arrived in his early 20s, Owen had never seen a film all the way through. Indeed, when taken on an England schoolboys' trip to watch the late John Candy in *Cool Runnings*, he confessed that he had struggled on through the first 10 minutes just to be polite, "then I shut my eyes and thought about football".

Owen later revealed that he was a fan of the television programme *Deal or No Deal* but worried as "the mystical aspects do my head in".

Meanwhile John Green, the consultant physiotherapist who helped Owen put together his 32-page brochure to prospective employers, revealed himself to be the new Nostradamus.

In it Green wrote: "The following are my thoughts on Michael Owen's so-called 'injury-prone' status – a statement I consider to be nonsense. Under my supervision Michael has not had any recurrence of his hamstring issues. In my opinion, he will play at the highest level for many years – trouble free!"

No. 18 BOBBY GOULD

After failing as Wales manager to such an extent that Blackwood boys the Manic Street Preachers used a Cardiff stadium gig to change the lyrics to their hit 'Everything Must Go' to "Bobby Gould must go", the silver-

"Coming up we'll speak to Coventry chairman Ray Ranson at the Rioja Arena..." – **RONNIE IRANI**

haired Max Clifford lookalike drifted into obscurity.

Until, brilliantly, *talkSPORT* hired him as a pundit. Some of his famous quotes are in this book and Gould has more than lived up to the early promise of his first broadcast, on which he declared: "I'm what you call a country pumpkin".

Other greatest hits: "The papers are portraying Rafa as a parrot, just like they did when they showed Graham Taylor as an onion", "Bob Lord was well reputated within the game", "Manchester United aren't as good as what they are", "They're living in land cuckoo land" and "United losing confirms Chelsea as the big containers now". Plus "Jamie O'Hara has been brilliant on the recordings I've seen of him on the radio" and the sensational "I've just been praising Dawson, then he makes a terrible pass. Hope I haven't put the plock on him."

Bobby went on to light up the 2010 World Cup, where he identified Dirk Kuyt as "Dick Van Dyke" and praised New Zealand with the words: "I've seen them go from the lowest ebb to the toppest ebb."

No. 17 DAVE WHELAN

The Wigan chairman loves to tell stories about his careful attitude to money. In a TV documentary, the former professional footballer and JJB Sports boss described how he helped out a warehouse employee with one sole hanging off his trainers. Whelan said he had reached into his pocket, pulled out a large wedge of cash... then given the wide-eyed lad the elastic band around it with the words "that should hold it on until payday". Oddly enough, exactly the same thing happened in an episode of *Only Fools and Horses*. Pure coincidence, of course.

No. 16 PHIL BROWN

Creosote of hue and with a pink jumper placed jauntily over his shoulders, Phil Brown's appearance on Sky Sports' *Goals on Sunday* in August 2009 was almost as alarming as Bywater's and arguably far worse than his infamous pitchside karaoke, alleged rescue of a suicidal woman on the Humber Bridge, half-time on-field team talk and claim that questions about his sunbed use were racist – "you wouldn't ask George Boateng that," he said. Sacked by Hull as they headed for relegation, some cruelly suggested he should keep his famous radio headset as it could be useful in his next job when he asked customers if they wanted fries with that. Shortly before his dismissal, he told an interviewer: "Any regrets? Loads. But I don't drink pints of hindsight, I drink pints of Guinness."

No. 15 **IAN HOLLOWAY**

A few years ago I spent an entire Plymouth Argyle matchday with Ian Holloway, arriving at his residence just as he finished his breakfast of a huge Cornish pastie.

Over the next few hours, Holloway clowned around, wearing joke glasses and showing off his giant "King Kong gloves" but also displayed meticulous preparation for that day's game and keen tactical acumen to go with his obvious motivational skills. As we were going down the tunnel from the dressing room, Holloway's sideman Des Bulpin pulled me over. "He wants you to think he's daft," said the former Spurs youth coach, "but you should know he's one of the cleverest men I've ever met in football."

It was a couple of days after Hallowe'en and I had no time to think about this comment when I turned left to the Plymouth bench to be greeted by the sight of one of the cleverest men in football, wearing a giant witch's hat emblazoned with silver stars and moons, sticking two thumbs up at me. "Oright boy?" he said.

In short, Holloway might be putting it on a bit, but who's arguing when you get quotes like these after a routine but ugly QPR win against Chesterfield: "To put it in gentleman's terms if you've been out for a night and you're looking for a young lady and you pull one, some weeks they're good looking and some weeks they're not the best. Our performance today would have been not the best-looking bird but at least we got her in the taxi. She weren't the best-looking lady we ended up taking home but she was very pleasant and very nice, so thanks very much, let's have a coffee."

137

No. 14 MANCHESTER UNITED FAN JOHN SIMPSON

Interviewed by a West Ham fanzine, the Manchester United supporter put up this sterling defence of his club:

Q: Do United fans prefer London games as you get home quicker after the match?

A: The only reason we get this label is because we are so well supported around the world, which you'd expect of such a great club.

Q: Where do you live?

A: Chigwell, Essex.

No. 13 LEE CROFT

As celebrated in Robbie Savage's fine weekly column for *MirrorFootball.co.uk*, the winger's culinary foibles include a love of sushi "but not the fish" and "Parmaham cheese".

Croft also believes that somewhere in the Arctic Circle is "a fly which flew the wrong way round the world and when it got there it just froze in the air, like an ice cube. It's still there to this day." He believes the government are working to suppress this knowledge.

Arranging to be picked up from his new rented house, Croft advised a club-mate that he couldn't remember his own door number but would leave a wheelybin outside the front door so they would know where to collect him. Naturally, they turned down Croft's road to discover it was bin day.

138

No. 12 ALAN BRAZIL

Easily the most entertaining broadcaster in Britain, the football-headed Scot is a delight to listen to on the occasions when he attends his own breakfast show on *talkSPORT*.

His own love of life and a good drink makes him shaky on the subjects of death and sobriety. Years ago, Brazil enquired after Bob Monkhouse's health only to be told by ashen-sounding pundit Gary Bushell that he died at Christmas. "I heard two

versions," replied our hero, brilliantly. When another celebrity passed away he paid a fulsome tribute to "TV's Inspector Morse, John Shaw". When his co-host pointed out that the actor's surname was Thaw, Brazil replied: "You know, I've been doing that all morning. John, if you're listening, sorry mate."

Brazil is also rightly famous for soliciting calls on "George Best's liver transplant and the booze culture in football" by advising listeners "don't forget, the best opinion wins a crate of John Smith's."

More recently, when Kenny Sansom shipped up to Alan Brazil's *talkSPORT* show to alcohol and gambling, the host interrupted to bring listeners "the latest odds from Coral" then, hearing Sansom would be signing his autobiography in London's Leadenhall Market, told him to "Get down Brokers wine bar while you're there, Kenny. On second thoughts, don't."

A national treasure, Brazil was once asked to name his favourite tipple. His reply? "God, there are so many..."

No. 11 NICK CHADWICK

The former Everton and Plymouth striker told his club's programme: "I'm a prankster. At parties, my favourite trick is to tell people I'm going to the toilet, then I just leave and go straight home."

CONTINUES P148

"I've got four words for you: Coppell for QPR. Hang on, that's not right. I'll check it... six words." – RONNIE IRANI

CHANTS IN A MILLION:
THE 25 BEST (NEWISH) FOOTBALL SONGS

The best chant I ever heard at football came when QPR upset then mighty Liverpool in 1989. To the tune of the then popular terrace favourite 'Elton John is a homosexual', the Rangers fans sang: 'Kenny Dalglish is incomprehensible'. These recent 25 are well up to that standard...

25) Blackburn fans, to the tune of 'Santa Claus is Coming to Town':
"You better watch out, you better beware, Good with his feet and great in the air, Santa Cruz is coming, To town."

24) Huddersfield fans, to the tune of 'On Top of Old Smokey':
"We've got Novak, We've got Novaaak. Our carpets are filthy. We've got Novak."

23) Liverpool fans, to the tune of 'Campione':
"We said his days were numbered, Now he plays here every week. We can't pronounce his surname, So we call him Nick the Greek. Oooh Kyrgiakos, the one and only, he is a loon."

22) Leeds fans, to the tune of 'Oh My God' by Kaiser Chiefs:
"Oh my God I can't believe it, We've never been this good away from home."

THE 3pm ANNUAL

"Get your players on who can unlock the door and sooner or later they will break the door down." – **TIM SHERWOOD**

"You can't turn a sow's ear into a rose. Or a flower." - MIKE PARRY

THE 30m ANNUAL

21) Leyton Orient fans, to the tune of 'Volare':
"Oh Churchie, whoah-oh, Churchie, whoah-oh-oh. His name suggests he's holy, He's going to beat your goalie!"

20) Portsmouth fans, to the tune of 'Que Sera Sera':
"King Kanu, Kanu. He's older than me and you. We all know he's 62. King Kanu, Kanu."

19) Manchester United fans, to the tune of 'Bad, Bad Leroy Brown':
"He's big, he's bad, he's Wesley Brown, The hardest man in all of town, Orange hair beware! Come and have a go if you dare."

18) Swindon fans, to the tune of 'Let It Be':
"When we find ourselves in times of trouble/Need to score a goal or three/ Wing the ball out wide to/MacNamee."

17) Ireland fans, to the tune of 'Molly Malone':
"Alive, alive-o-oh, Alive, alive-o-oh, Stephen Ireland's two grannies. Alive, alive-o!"

16) Aston Villa fans, to the tune of 'Happy Days':
"Sunday, Monday, Habib Beye. Tuesday, Wednesday, Habib Beye. Thursday, Friday, Habib Beye. Saturday, Habib Beye, rocking all week with you."

15) **Stoke fans, to the tune of 'Too Shy':**
"Tun-cay-cay, Huth Huth, Abdoulaye."

14) **Tottenham fans, to the tune of 'Son Of My Father':**
"Oh, Benny, Benny/ Benny, Benny, Assou Hyphen Ekotto."

13) **Manchester United fans, to the tune of 'Lord Of The Dance':**

"Kaka, wherever you may be, Have you heard of Man City? Don't go there, It'll end in tears. They've not won a trophy in 30 years."

12) **Fulham fans, to the tune of 'Lord of the Dance':**
"Chelsea, whoever you may be/You've been done by a Conspiracy/Barca drew, so they go through/To a final wanted by Platini."

11) **Crystal Palace fans, to the tune of 'I Will Always Love You':**
"N'Diayee-i-ee-i will always love you."

10) **Liverpool fans, to the tune of 'Hello Goodbye':**
"N'Gog N'Go. I don't know why you say N'Gog I say N'Go."

9) **Northern Ireland fans, to the tune of 'Yellow Polka Dot Bikini':**
"We've got an itsy-bitsy, teeny-weeny, baldy-headed Warren Feeney."

"Bob Lord was well reputated within the game." – **BOBBY GOULD**

8) **Fulham fans, to the tune of 'That's Amore':**
"When the ball hits your head/And you're sat in Row Z/That's Zamora."

7) **Liverpool fans, to the tune of 'Rhythm is a Dancer':**
"Benny is a dancer, skipping past defenders, Benayoun is everywhere."

6) **Manchester City fans, to the tune of 'This Old Man':**
"U-N-I-T-E-D, That spells f***ing debt to me, With a knick knack paddywhack, give a dog a bone, Ocean Finance on the phone."

5) **Fulham fans, to the tune of 'Bread of Heaven':**
"Brede Hange-land, Brede Hange-land, He is Norway's Bobby Moore (Bobby Moore). He is Norway's Bobby Moore."

4) **Liverpool fans, to the tune of 'He Shot, He Missed':**
"He's small, he's red, he's got an outsize head. Joey Cole, Joey Cole."

3) **Chelsea fans, to the tune of 'He Shot, He Missed':**
"He's rich, they're Scouse, they're going to rob his house. Joey Cole, Joey Cole."

143

2) **Everton fans, to the tune of 'You're So Vain':**
"Leighton Baines – I bet you think this song is about you."

1) **Fulham fans, to the tune of 'Black Betty':**
"Oh Big Brede (Hangeland), Whoah, big Brede (Hangeland), He jumps so high (Hangeland), You know that's no lie (Hangeland), He's so rock steady (Hangeland), When you see him on telly (Hangeland), Oh Big Brede (Hangeland), Whoah big Brede (Hangelaaaaaand)."

PUZZLE TIME

Can you solve these mathematical football teasers?

1) A train full of United fans is travelling from London to Manchester. The distance between Euston and Piccadilly stations is 160 miles. If the train travels at an average speed of 90mph, how long will they be travelling on the day in question?

Answer: *Four hours. The journey to Manchester will take 120 minutes. But after the match the United fans will have to return to their homes in the South. Note: This calculation does not take into account connecting trains to Bournemouth.*

2) At the Emirates Stadium, Nathan buys a chorizo sausage in an artisan bread roll for 7. His friend Clive buys three grande hazelnut lattes with a 20 note and receives 8 change. Their friend Jonathan buys himself and Clive each a tray of line-caught cod in Adnams Beer Batter, served with chunkily chipped Lady Balfour potatoes. Each costs 7.50. Assuming the cost of sale is 20 per cent and a further 25 per cent of the gross goes on general administration, how much will the friends have contributed towards buying a new goalkeeper for Arsene Wenger?

Answer: *Nothing. Wenger will refuse to buy a goalkeeper, preferring instead to pick up a geriatric Basque and a promising Swiss 16-year-old on free transfers.*

3) England footballer X has broken off his affair with model P. She is threatening to tell all to the press. If obtaining a superinjunction will take his lawyers 2.5 days at 35,000 per day how much must he pay to ensure everything ends amicably?

Answer: *244,500. The superinjunction will cost 87,500 but will not work and once news of their relationship leaks, X's agent J will meet model P at an Essex health spa with a cheque for 75,000 to buy her continuing silence. X will then take wife Y to Barbados to renew their wedding vows, costing a further 68,000. Meanwhile he will need to buy second mistress Q Dior jewellery worth 14,000 to keep her sweet until he returns home.*

144

"What Ron Atkinson said was unforgiveable. Although, in time, we should forgive him." – **MIKE PARRY**

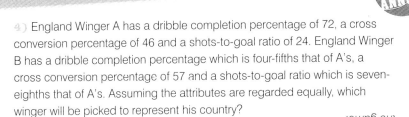

4) England Winger A has a dribble completion percentage of 72, a cross conversion percentage of 46 and a shots-to-goal ratio of 24. England Winger B has a dribble completion percentage which is four-fifths that of A's, a cross conversion percentage of 57 and a shots-to-goal ratio which is seven-eighths that of A's. Assuming the attributes are regarded equally, which winger will be picked to represent his country?

Answer: Neither. Winger A and Winger B will both lose out to David Beckham, who will be picked because he is a great ambassador for the game.

5) Striker E talks at a rate of 90 words per minute. Midfielder F talks at a rate of 50 words per minute. E has promised to speak to a journalist for two minutes after the match, while F has promised the hack five minutes of his time. Which footballer uses the most words?

Answer: Player E, with two. After their side is defeated, he says "sorry, mate" to the journalist and pretends to be fiddling with his phone as he walks through the mixed zone and gets onto the team coach. Meanwhile Player F dons sunglasses and massive headphones and strolls through without a word.

6) Player N is late to meet his girlfriend for lunch. The local pay and display car park is four minutes from the restaurant and costs a flat fee of 4 for 3 hours' parking. Meters 90 seconds from the restaurant cost 1.50 per hour but will need refilling every 60 minutes. What does N choose to save time and money?

145

Answer: He parks in the disabled bay outside the restaurant, having earned 10 times the possible fine while having his starter.

THE 50 MADDEST FOOTBALL VIDEOS... EVER CONTINUED

5) Fergie talks gibberish

Sir Alex Ferguson had clearly been enjoying himself at the races when the cameras caught up with him. What follows makes more sense than he usually does...

Search Vimeo.com for "Hic, Cheers" or go to http://bit.ly/c2TBfH

146

4) "I no speak England very very well mate"

We love Manchester United's Anderson. Not only does he look vaguely like Rolf from *The Muppet Show*, but this interview with MUTV, in which he bravely speaks English despite not being very good at it, is a classic in which he names "Ass Brown" as one of his team-mates and declares: "I am big prove".

Search for "Interview with Anderson" or go to http://bit.ly/Td4XO

3) A quiet night in Liverpool

One of the few good things about England in the 2010 World Cup, this

brilliant clip shows Phil Thompson, live from a function in Liverpool, telling Sky how proud everyone on Merseyside is to see Scouser Steven Gerrard captain England. "It's been a great night, everybody's enjoyed it," says the Concorde-beaked pundit. Well, perhaps not quite everybody...

Search for "Phil Thompson background" or go to http://bit.ly/bYd8Bc

2) Tornado hits game

What are the worst conditions you've ever played football in? Gloves-on cold? Bit of drizzle? Have a look at this from Japan. We think the match might just have been abandoned.

Search for "Soccer tornado" or go to http://bit.ly/agmFGT

1) Fainting commentator

Brazilian TV pundit Bastista takes a deep breath around 0:28 of this bit of post-match analysis. What happens next is truly shocking. Luckily, he was OK.

Search for "Comentarista Batista" or go to http://bit.ly/cKNUD3

THE 100 MADDEST PEOPLE IN FOOTBALL
CONTINUED

No. 10 DIEGO MARADONA

Where to begin with the drug-snorting, hand-balling, cigar-puffing, Castro-worshipping, ephedrine-taking wild man whose original nickname in Argentina was... "Fluffy"?

When a paunchy, wild-eyed Maradona entered a Cuban psychiatric clinic in early 2004 to combat his drug addiction, the football world breathed a sigh of relief. It took a sharp intake of breath a few months later when photos emerged of the 43-year-old in rehab, one showing him snorting cocaine and another depicting the Hand of God cheat having sex with 19-year-old Cuban girlfriend Adonay Fruto, in front of several admiring onlookers.

It says something about the shock value of the first two snaps that a third, showing the tubby hand-baller dressed up as Osama bin Laden and wielding a toy machine gun, caused many a raised eyebrow.

Maradona excelled as Argentina coach at the 2010 World Cup, possibly in spite of himself.

Having done his bit for press relations by telling his critics to "suck it and keep on sucking it", he proved his sound judgement by attempting to appoint former international team-mate Oscar "The Big-Headed One" Ruggeri as his assistant in January. Ruggeri's recent coaching exploits had included Tecos UAG in Mexico (resigned after losing his first six games) and Spain's Elche (sacked after 20 games), plus Argentine sides Independiente (lasted four months, quit after being booed by fans at a home game) and San Lorenzo (sacked following 7-1 home defeat to Boca Juniors).

His appointment was blocked by the country's FA.

> "The Champions League semi-final is over two legs, so it will be a one-off affair." – **GRAHAM BEECROFT**

No. 9 THE RAPID VIENNA BIRDWATCHER

Neo-Nazism is, alas, still alive and well on the terraces of Austria. Hence, after hearing a supporter had taunted Hapoel Tel Aviv fans with a "Hitler salute" during a European match, the court refused to accept his explanation that he had "merely been pointing out a rare Peregrine Falcon to a friend". He was banned from the ground for three years.

No. 8 RODNEY MARSH

Dumped by Sky Sports for making a joke about the Asian Tsunami, Marsh went on to a bewildering career at *talkSPORT*, where, once on air he responded to his co-host's enquiry about what he'd done over the weekend with the words: "I was down on the coast and I thought about suicide again. Ultimately I would have to say I am very depressed right now and if there are any psychiatrists listening could they call me and give me some advice?"

Later he shared this cheery tale with readers of his blog: "Yesterday at 4am my neighbour took his nickel-plated 45 handgun and blew his brains on to his General Electric fridge. I was chatting with him in the driveway the night before. He didn't sound too happy, but that was a bit radical."

It wasn't all doom and gloom on Marsh's sadly discontinued internet diary, however. Readers were also treated to in-depth discussions of his bowel movements, including this magnificent – ahem – passage: "Saturday: Been a bit constipated since I got back from the States. Wednesday morning: Four days. It's the change in water I think. Had loads of bran and fruit for breakfast and hot tea... no luck. Thursday: Had a lovely hot cup of tea and a great 'Eartha'. Felt like I was giving birth to an adult anaconda."

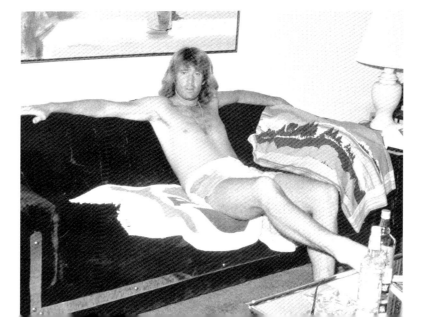

No. 7 GEORGE GILLETT

Liverpool's popular co-owner hinted at his inaugural press conference that all might not go smoothly when he told reporters: "My son Foster is a fan of soccer. He was a goaltender. His brother was a defenseman."

Arsenal suitor Alisher Uzmanov made a similar remark when he laid out his football fan credentials with the words: "I fell in love with the game in 1966, when the Great British national team won over the Germans."

No. 6 VINNIE JONES

"My goal is an Oscar. It has to be," insisted the nose-biting "Welshman" early in his movie career. Since then he has starred in *The Comdemned*, *The Heavy*, *The Bleeding*, *Midnight Meat Train*, *Return of the Ripper*, *Hell Ride* and *Garfield 2: A Tail Of Two Kitties*. He has played characters called Mongrel, Cain, Brick, Zed, Gunnar, Hunter, Billy Wings and Smasher O'Driscoll. Yet he still awaits recognition from the Academy of Motion Picture Arts and Sciences.

Though a reality TV show venture proved disappointing – BBC3's *Vinnie* attracted just 10,000 viewers a week – Jones has had success in the pop world. In 2007 Vinnie contributed a stunning spoken-word track to soul Wurzel Joss Stone's CD *Introducing Joss Stone*. The lyrics included these wise words: "I know change/I see change/I embody change... We are born to change/We sometimes regard it as a metaphor/That reflects the way/Fings ought to be." "She'd have been better advised to have a monologue from Fred West fronting the album," gushed the *Guardian*, while London's *Evening Standard* hailed his contribution as "pathetic drivel".

In 2002 Vinnie recorded his own album, *Respect*, featuring him reinterpreting soul classics like 'Dock of the Bay', 'In the Midnight Hour' and 'Bad, Bad Leroy Brown'. One customer review on Amazon.com reads: "This

"Alex McLeish has just had his hands in his head." – **CHRIS KAMARA**

"No matter how much you're expecting it, the sack is still unexpected." – **JASON McATEER**

"The Arsenal youth team is full of young players." – **ROBBIE EARLE**

is the greatest album I have ever heard. Vinnie Jones makes Gandhi look like a pornographer."

Vinnie says he talks to his grandfather "almost every day". Alas, Arthur Jones died in 1977.

No. 5 ROMARIO

At the end of his career, the Brazilian legend gave a magazine his top 10 tips for aspiring footballers. And you had to say they were a step up from the usual "try to work on your weaker foot... keep your head down and listen to advice from the coaches".

Number one? "Find a p***k to slag you off and motivate yourself with this challenge." Number six? "Dream like f**k." And number seven: "Shag every day. Three times at the most."

No. 4 SIR ALEX FERGUSON

A genius manager, a good socialist, a tireless charity worker and a miserable, curmudgeonly old git. My *Daily Mirror* boss Dean Morse once asked Fergie what he could do to repair the paper's fragile relationship with Old Trafford. "You could try dying," came the conciliatory response. The last time I saw Sir Alex in the flesh he was berating Jeff Stelling in front of

152

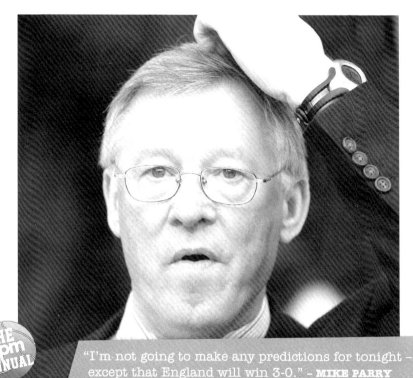

the entire Football Writers' Association for asking Wayne Rooney – who'd just won an award – a completely innocuous question about Paul Scholes. Then, of course, there was this famous, unbroadcast, exchange with Sky's Geoff Shreeves over a similarly harmless query to Cristiano Ronaldo:

Shreeves: I asked him...

Ferguson: F***ing (inaudible) bastard.

Shreeves: Don't talk to me like that.

Ferguson: F**k off to you.

Shreeves: Don't talk to me like that. Don't even think about it.

Ferguson: Don't you think about it, you ****. F**k off. Right?

Shreeves: Listen, are you going to do the interview in a professional manner or not? Do you want to do it or not?

Ferguson: You f*****g be professional. You be professional. You're the one.

Shreeves: I'm entitled to ask... Cristiano gave the right answer.

Ferguson: F***ing hell with your answers.

Shreeves: Don't talk to me like that. Go away. If you want to behave civilly, fine. Don't talk to me like that.

Ferguson: F**k off.

Let's not forget the boot kicked into poor David Beckham's brow – is that why he looks permanently startled these days, or could it be something else? – and its precursor when Fergie was the boss at lowly St Mirren. One old boy remembered: "Alex kicked out at someone's sports bag and a pair of underpants floated up out of it and landed on the substitute's head.

"The lad was so scared he just sat there with a pair of Y-fronts over his face as Alex kept on ranting. After five minutes he stormed out and slammed the dressing room door. Then 10 seconds later it opened again and he roared: 'And you! Get those f***ing underpants off your head.'"

No. 3 MIKE PARRY

A former tabloid journalist and FA official, the diminutive, portly, ginger, bespectacled Parry is one of British football's leading thinkers.

153

154

When not turning his attention to other sports – where he has campaigned to have ejector seats installed in Formula 1 cars and for race horses to be fitted with wing mirrors – the Everton fan has called for referees to use Segway vehicles to speed around the pitch, and also proposed a radical solution to the question of whether the Premier League should introduce American football-style instant replays. Parry said that he feared the red flags thrown by NFL coaches would be easily overlooked in the hurly-burly of a match, so instead suggested that "each manager should have an orange balaclava in their pocket and when they want to protest a decision they have to put it on". A listener called to say that this would be a problem in the case of Phil Brown, who already looks to be wearing a full-face orange balaclava.

A history buff, Mike often treats listeners to discussions of "when Wellington won the Battle of Trafalgar", "the Bordeaux Tapestry" or "Oxford's rumbling spires". He is also a natural with the station's listeners, and there were tantalizing hints of a Scottish remake of Harrison Ford film *Witness* when Mike asked a caller who refused to buy a TV set whether he was "one of the Hamish".

"That was the perfect penalty, apart from he missed it." - **ROB McCAFFREY**

There was this quiz question, powered by Parry's mispronunciation of Ireland's manager...

PARRY: How many Os are there in Trappatini?

CALLER: One.

PARRY: Correct.

As well as this slightly tricky exchange…

PARRY: "Where are you ringing from?"

CALLER: "Rothley in Leicestershire – the home of the McCanns."

PARRY: "What, the famous oven chips?"

CALLER: "No, the parents of little Maddy."

PARRY: "Oh."

He also took a memorable call from a man in Wales who, it emerged, lived near Parry's elderly auntie. There followed several moments of on-air visit planning before the great man remembered she was dead ("and I apologize to all concerned").

Parry is perhaps at his finest, however, on an outside broadcast. Belfast for England v Northern Ireland was memorable ("there goes a police car... or 'The Pigs', as they used to call them here during the Troubles") and so was this summer's jaunt to South Africa ("this is the time that the country of South Africa finally pulls itself together and becomes the Rainbow Nation, a rainbow of peace... and... quiet"). But never to be forgotten is his reportage from the Manchester United v Chelsea Champions League final in Moscow, when Mike phoned into Ian Collins' post-midnight show having enjoyed the hospitality.

"To start off with, you're a cultured man, you're a libero or something," began Parry, sensibly. "What I'm saying to you is you can't escape the redness, the liberalism of the former Communist Party in Moscow. The greatest thing about Moscow is... that it's Moscow. The Americans call it Mos-cow but it shouldn't be called that, because it's not a cow, it's Mos-coe. I'm walking now into an area of mist. I've just gone into the early morning air of Moscow and (sings tuneless approximation of theme to *M*A*S*H**) 'In early morning mist I see, lots of things and misery'... You see, the difference between you and me, Ian, is that I see there are winners and losers in life. (Sings approximation of Abba song) 'The winner takes it all... the loser takes... a fall'... That's what I'm saying to you. You and I have worked together sometimes. And sometimes without. But you're a better man than I. And I'm in Moscow, which is a third world country, and you're at *talkSPORT*, which is a magnificent station and a magnificent country..."

Wonderful.

155

No. 2 ASHLEY COLE

Where did it all go wrong for the finest left-back England have produced in decades? The Boveyesque lottery picture? The breathtaking arrogance of his autobiography *My Defence*, in which Cole admitted he "nearly swerved off the road" when he heard Arsenal were offering him only £55,000-a-week ("'He is taking the piss, Jonathan,' I yelled down the phone. I was so incensed. I was trembling with anger")? The vomit-strewn romp with hairdresser Aimee Walton? The ill-advised mobile phone addiction which finally ended his marriage to brave little songbird/national treasure Chezza? The message to mates which read: "I hate England and all the people"?

Hard to know where Ashley goes from here in his quest to become the greatest British sporting villain since Giant Haystacks. Will he make a prank phone call to Andrew Sachs? Announce that malaria is "not that big a deal"? Claim to have been driving a white Fiat Uno in Paris on August 31, 1997? And surely the announcement of his starring role in a hilarious new football TV show, co-starring James Corden, can't be far away...

156

THE 3pm ANNUAL

No. 1 STEPHEN IRELAND

The mental midfielder in the Superman underpants first rose to prominence while trying to dodge Northern Ireland duty in 2007 with the genius excuse that his grandmother had died. When the bewildered lady in question denied being dead, Ireland claimed it was his other grandma who'd gone toes-up. She too popped up, still breathing normally. "I would like to apologize to my grandmothers for any distress I have caused them," he said.

Eager to learn more about this special young talent, reporters then came across his Facebook page, on which Ireland had opined that "football is shit, why did I get stuck doin it?", nicknamed himself "Daddy Dick" and listed his favourite things in life thus:

MUSIC: R. Kelly is all iv t say, fast RnB Music Storch-Hot!!!!, and a bit of barneys rhymes N Jackson 5 wit The Big Man then ya know.

MOST UPSET WHEN: i lose at pro evo, which isnt very often, battered every contestant dat came my way, recent loser. PAUL REIDY, There Was Lessons Thrown His Way. Bummer!!!!!!!"

In 2008, Ireland celebrated his part in the City's first derby win at Old Trafford since 1974 by buying a £90,000 Range Rover and fitting it with shocking pink wheels and grille. His other automotive misdemeanours are listed elsewhere in this book.

157

Having sported a clearly receding hairline the previous season, Ireland appeared at the start of the new campaign with a suspiciously luxurious thatch. Later, being Ireland, he shaved it all off.

In 2010 Ireland moved into a new £5m mansion in the footballers' enclave of Prestbury and installed a new home aquarium, holding 6,000 litres of saltwater – 75 times more than an average aquarium and featuring a reef imported from Fiji.

Not willing to rest on his laurels, Ireland then told friends he planned to dig up his tiled kitchen floor and replace it with glass. Under that, he hoped to build a giant fish tank... with a shark in it.

THE 3pm ANNUAL

PUZZLE **ANSWERS**

Page 14

(O3, W) SIRALEXFERGUSON
(C7, S) ABRUPT
(C7, E) ABUSIVE
(F5, E) HAIRDRYER
(E9, N) BLUNT
(I9, SE) BOORISH
(F8, E) CHURLISH
(E3, SE) GRACELESS
(H16, N) GRUFF
(P7, W) IMPOLITE
(B12, SE) SURLY
(P4, S) UNCIVIL
(B10, N) UNGRACIOUS
(G16, NE) BRUSQUE
(I15, NW) RUDDY
(D11, S) FLORID
(E12, SW) GOVAN
(J16, NE) AGEING
(F16, NE) YOUSE
(I10, SW) PERCH
(P9, SW) IDIOTS
(D7, NW) BBC
(L10, W) STOPWATCH
(D4, E) BURGUNDY
(A2, S) INTIMIDATING
(D1, SE) FERGIETIME
(L2, W) MINDGAMES

Page 60

A; Michael Essien; B: Cristiano Ronaldo, C: Lee Sharpe, D: Dwight Yorke, E: El-Hadji Diouf, F: Jermaine Jenas, G: Shaun Wright-Phillips, H: Rio Ferdinand, I: Ronaldinho, J: Diego Maradona, K: Ashley Cole, L: Cristiano Ronaldo, M: Nigel Quashie, N: John Terry

159